THE
Other Side
OF NAM

IKE TRAVIS

outskirts
press

Dedication:

To my dear late wife, Manette Belliveau.
This book would have never been written
without your belief in me.
Thank you so much!

ACKNOWLEDGMENT:

To all Vietnam veterans: From being in Vietnam, you may or may not relate to all of my stories, but you may relate to some of it as we all have our own unique Vietnam stories.

TABLE OF CONTENTS

CHAPTER 1

LIVE OAK IS a small, agricultural community located in Northern California on the east side of the Sutter Buttes. At the time, Live Oak had a little over two thousand people who called it home. My name is Ike Travis, and I was one of those fortunate people. Live Oak now boasts a population of over eight thousand. Everyone enjoyed warm summer nights and crisp winters. Farmers loved the warm weather, which was ideal for raising crops in the Sacramento Valley. Our community was from another era where everyone attended the same schools and pretty much knew everyone else.

My mom (Georgia) grew up in Live Oak. Her mom had died in childbirth, and her father disappeared. She was given away and raised by a wonderful couple, William and Mabel McTyer, who were unable to have children. William had retired from the US Navy, where he was a pharmacist for twenty years, spending most of his duty among small Asian islands. He later worked at the US Post Office in Live Oak as the postmaster. Mabel was a registered nurse.

Sadly, I never met Grandpa Mac, and Grandma Mabel passed away when I was only twelve years old.

Mom worked as a grocery checker at King's Market, one of the only grocery stores in town, and became an accomplished pianist, playing and singing for several local churches during the Christmas holidays. With her blue eyes, blond hair, and petite frame, all the men in town loved her and her voice.

Dad was part Cherokee Indian, and as a young boy, lived on a reservation in Kentucky. He worked in construction and was also a jeweler/watchmaker and owned a small jewelry store in town. He would come home from his carpentry work and spend evenings repairing watches.

During the late 1920s, he traveled from Kentucky to California, and I always enjoyed hearing his stories of how he and his sisters survived the Depression and made the journey in a Model A Ford. He was only fourteen when he made the drive with his sixteen- and seventeen-year-old sisters, Lorean and Rosie. Dad (Arvell Travis) quit school at age twelve to work full time with his father in construction and was driving by age thirteen.

Dad was a boxer and would fight for money. His father taught him to box at a very young age and used to practice with him in the evenings. My two aunts would hustle money from men at the bar and hold the money during the fights. Other times, they would just steal the money and leave town before the match. They would do almost anything in order to fund the journey. Dads fighting ended in Pocatello, Idaho, when he took a beating so bad that he never wanted to fight again! Dad used to joke about his sisters never running out of money. They were truly Flapper Girls and good at it.

I also learned to box at a very young age. Dad enjoyed teaching me and loved to show off his boxing skills. I was not real big but pretty fast. Dad frequently said, "It's not the size of the man, but the speed." He was only five foot nine with a thin build but had very strong arms. He said the guy that beat him in Pocatello was even smaller than he was but was as fast as lightning.

I grew up in the same house as my mom. We had an outhouse until

I was eight years old. It was located about fifty feet from the back of the house on a dirt path. My dad would always remind us kids at night, on our way to the outhouse, to watch out for "old raw head and bloody bones." Dad loved to tell spooky stories.

My childhood was wonderful. Farmland and orchards surrounded our house in the country. A few miles east of town is the Feather River, where I spent many enjoyable hours partying with family and friends. I grew up hunting, fishing, camping, and going to church. As a young boy, I was raised as a Presbyterian until the church closed in Live Oak when I was about twelve years old. My father was always a Mormon (Church of the Latter Day Saints), so we all took the lessons and became Mormons going to the church in Gridley, just north of Live Oak, about seven miles. Our family was very loving and did many things together. Being the only son with a sister, Arvella, and two half sisters, Gloria and Nadine, I was probably a bit spoiled. I was the youngest. Both Gloria and Nadine were married and gone by the time I was born, so it was just Arvella and I at home. Gloria married Robert Turner, and Nadine married Jerry Saunders.

I learned to cook very young because everyone had chores, and if you cook, you didn't have to clean. My corn fritters were the best, if I do say so myself.

For my eighth-grade graduation present from my mom and dad, I received a Ruger Bearcat .22 pistol—my very first pistol, and I was twelve years old.

Dad loved to target practice with me, but he would always use his Smith & Wesson .357 Magnum. We would practice together at least once a week unless we were hunting. We would set up targets behind our house that was surrounded by prune orchards.

Richard Wilson was my closest neighbor. We could walk through his dad's prune orchard to reach each other's houses.

When other boys had bicycles at age thirteen, both Richard and I had Honda 50s. We would ride through the orchards almost every evening. Sometimes, we would sneak into town, about five miles away.

We would always try to get home before dark; avoiding the bums we would see walking the canals, which fed the orchards and farms in Live Oak. They always scared us, even though most were harmless.

One night, we noticed one of the farmers had just picked up his walnuts, and they were all there in large bags. Kenny, my cousin, came over to spend the night, and the three of us decided to go back after dark and take one of the bags. We figured it must be worth about twenty dollars, and who would ever notice one missing bag? It took hours for us to sneak into his yard and grab a bag and then carry it all the way home. After a couple of hours of carrying the large bag, we hid it behind Richard's neighbor's tractor.

The next morning when the owner of the tractor noticed it, he knew right away where it came from, as he was also a County Sheriff. The next thing I knew, a police car came down my driveway with Richard and Kenny in the backseat. He put me in the backseat as well and told my mom he would bring me back later. He then drove us, and the bag of walnuts, back to the farmer's house. The farmer told us because he knew my parents and Richard's parents very well that he would not press charges if we apologized and never stole from him again. We were terrified, but we all apologized.

Richard loved to hunt. He hunted both pheasant and deer with Dad and me. He hunted doves with another neighbor and ducks with his grandpa. He really did like to hunt.

On one of many hunting and camping trips, as I was sleeping in the back of Dad's 1958 Ford truck, I was awakened by a gunshot. Richard was in the front seat with Dad and just made a shot straight down a canyon. We were in the High Sierras outside of Washington, California. Richard just shot his first deer. He was so excited. Me? I was not so excited when I realized the deer was about one hundred yards *straight down*. It took us hours to get the deer up to the truck. At times, we would pull the deer up by a rope, and we would all slip back down.

Then, we had to clean it. Richard wanted to do it himself, but Dad had to finish the job because Richard pierced the colon with his knife and almost ruined the rest of the meat. Dad knew what to do and cleaned it up. That night for dinner around the campfire, we all ate fresh venison liver with onions. It was excellent, and it was always fun talking around the campfire.

I was a year behind Arvella in school. It was difficult because the teachers expected me to be an A student like her. I did do well in some classes, but I had to work for it, and it always seemed so easy for her.

Being an average student in high school, I was very pleased when I came up to the top of my second year of typing class, able to type seventy-four words per minute on a standard typewriter. I felt like an unofficial teacher's assistant. I would always help the new girls. I loved timed typing tests. It was so much fun showing off.

During my teenage years, weekends were spent either camping with my parents or partying with my neighbor, Richard, and my cousin, Kenny Denney, at the river. Even though the three of us had other school friends, we usually got together for Saturday night at the Feather River. If we didn't have a river party, we would all meet at the drive-in theater in Marysville. (Kenny was actually the son of my mom's aunt, but she and Mom were about the same age, and Kenny only a few months older than I was.)

It was very easy to get beer, even at our age. We would just drive to downtown Marysville and get any bum to buy us beer. The south end of town was the sleazy part, and we could always count on a bum standing there waiting for a handout. A bum is what we called men who just stood around on the corners all day. It was normal to buy him a six-pack of beer or a bottle of wine for his trouble.

We would go to the Feather River in the evening, build a fire, and party. The river could be swift in places, so we were all very careful when swimming. Sometimes, we had hot dogs and marshmallows for the campfire. We kept the fires small as we were usually trespassing on some farmer's land. There was very little access to the river without trespassing, but we knew where to go. Especially Richard as he knew most all of the farmers.

I was fortunate to inherit my mother's musical talents, so I learned to play the guitar and played a little at some of our river parties. Kenny also played guitar and would also play at times.

I played in a band during my freshman year in high school, along with several others from school. We called ourselves Acorn. In those days, we were playing songs like "Louie Louie" and "House of the Rising Sun." Not very good, but we sure had fun.

John and Marcia from Yuba City always joined the fun. Marcia had a lovely voice and sang almost every weekend. Everyone loved to hear Marcia sing!

Kenny lived in Marysville and would sometimes bring along a couple of girls from Marysville High. Richard would bring girls from Sutter as he had several friends there. We encouraged anyone that showed up to bring more friends. Sometimes, the river parties would get quite large as the word spread.

The parties were seldom in the same locations as we tried our best not to get caught. Even though we considered ourselves party animals, Richard, Kenny, and I did not do any drugs. We did drink a little beer, had big laughs, and a great time. Sometimes maybe too much beer.

It was a time that I felt well liked by my classmates and connected to the community. When the group whittled down toward the end of the party, many of the late-night conversations would end up being about graduation and the Vietnam War. Vietnam was a major topic during this time. The music, the demonstrations, and the news all had a tremendous impact on everyone. Graphic, violent scenes of the war were televised for the first time in America's living rooms. It was a lot to process as a teen, and these occasions allowed us to talk about our concerns at a safe distance.

There was an innocence at this time, with none of us knowing what the future would be.

THE OTHER SIDE OF NAM

CHAPTER 2

DURING MY HIGH school years, I would work evenings at a Shell gas station in Yuba City, about twenty minutes south of Live Oak. My mother had been opposed to me working alone at night, but my father reasoned that it was part of growing up.

One night, working at the station, I helped a customer at the gas pump. It was almost closing time, and no other cars were around. I headed back into the office to sit on the tall stool behind the counter where the cash register, cigarettes, and candy bars were displayed. A man a few years older than I had silently followed me inside and now leaned on the other side of the counter.

"Two packs of Marlboros," he said. As I turned around to pull the cigarettes from the display shelves, I heard a swishing sound as the man pulled a handgun that he had hidden in the back of his jeans. I was stunned to see the barrel of the gun pointed at me over the counter.

"Open the register!" he demanded.

It wasn't the money. I had no problem handing over what cash was in the box. Each twenty, or larger bills collected, were immediately stuffed down the slot in the floor safe for just such an occasion. However, during my brief training by the owner, I just never dreamed there would be a robbery.

The robber was about twenty-five years old with a couple of days old beard. His eyes were bloodshot, and his hands were shaking as he held the gun. That is what scared me the most. He could be desperate enough to really shoot me for the money.

Greedily, the robber stuffed the odd assortment of small bills into his jeans pockets and then told me to go into the lube room. I said, "No." I felt that if I went into the lube room where I wouldn't be seen that he would kill me. He said, "Turn around! Close your eyes. If you open them, I'll blow your head off."

The robber pulled the office door shut, and I heard him run past the gas pumps and into the night. I heard his footsteps running to the right, so I took off down the street in the opposite direction. I sure didn't want him coming back to check on me. Although I later identified the robber's photo at the police station, the police never arrested him.

About a month later, he appeared again late at night. He was standing in the office, waiting for me to finish helping another customer. He looked just as ragged as I remembered, only worse this time. I didn't let him know that I had recognized him. I told him that I would be there in just a few minutes.

The person I was helping with gas was shocked when I told him what was going on. He said, "Get in the car now, and we'll drive off." He drove me directly to the police station. By the time I got back to the gas station with the police, the robber had fled.

Again, I pointed him out in a photo album at the police station, but again, they didn't arrest him. I never knew why.

I continued to work at the gas station until I left my parents home, but always in fear. Kenny heard later that the police were afraid of the robber's family, as they were associated with the Mafia on the East

Coast. I wondered if this was true.

Richard spread the word throughout Yuba City and Sutter that we were looking for the robber. He thought we should find him and beat him to a pulp. I really didn't want to see him ever again.

CHAPTER 3

RICHARD WAS QUITE the scrapper when he was young. His dad was very mean to him and would beat Richard. Richard's response to this was to get into fights in school, and he always seemed to win, no matter how big his opponents were. One guy, in particular, Jeff, paid the price. He picked a fight with Richard and tried to embarrass him. He was so much bigger than Richard and two years ahead in school. Jeff was a senior, and Richard only a sophomore. Richard stood about five foot eleven and weighed 150 pounds. Jeff was about six-two and weighed around 200 pounds.

They met after school in the back of the gym for the fight. Jeff came at Richard, and Richard only swung once. In the auto shop that afternoon, Richard had made what looked like brass knuckles, but they were made of plastic, about six inches around. He held it in his right hand. It reminded me of a small bowling ball. Jeff fell to the ground, immediately covered in blood. He had to be rushed to the hospital for multiple stitches. The school called the police, but nothing ever happened because Richard said he only hit Jeff with his fist. The weapon was never located. Richard later told me that the ball went into the river. Jeff never bothered Richard again.

During my high school years, Live Oak High School hired a new principal, Mr. Andreason, a very nice man, tall and slender, who loved sports. He also had a son, Rusty, who was one year ahead of me in school and very athletic.

In my junior year, my PE class was playing baseball. The instructor was a substitute teacher, Mr. Nelson. Mr. Nelson was your typical sports coach . . . cocky, big, and loud. The batter hit the ball, and it flew high up into the blue sky. Out in the field, I began running where I thought it would come down. The sun in my eyes made it impossible to follow the ball's path, and another fielder and I collided. He was much larger, ran over me, and knocked me to the grass in excruciating pain.

Mr. Nelson yelled from the sideline, "Get up; get up!"

My arms were unable to push me off the ground. I did not understand what had happened. The pain was horrible. Seeing my futile efforts to roll to my side and sit up, Mr. Nelson added, "Ah, come on. You're faking it. Get up."

Luckily, Richard was just coming into gym class. Realizing that I was badly hurt, he ran out onto the field and scooped me up. He was going to carry me to his car to go for medical help. Almost immediately, Richard had to drop me. Doug, the big guy that ran over me, intercepted him. Pushing, shoving, and then an all-out fistfight resulted. Both Richard and Doug were throwing punches, and Doug went down. Richard picked me up again and headed for the car. We had to go through the gym to get to the parking lot.

Mr. Nelson was yelling at Richard to stop. I think he was embarrassed with all of the fighting going on.

As we reached the gymnasium's double doors, they opened up, and the next class of boys came blindly stampeding in. One in the crowd (Jimmy, a senior) accidentally slammed into us and caused us to fall. Richard left me on the cement, and he and Jimmy started yelling at each other. The rest of the class stopped and formed a circle to watch. It all happened so fast. A fight broke out, and Richard and Jimmy were both throwing punches. Some of the crowd stopped the fight by pulling each of them back. Richard picked me up again and continued through the gym. On the far side, we exited the building. Then Richard carried me to his car and drove to the hospital. There was no hospital in Live Oak, so we had to go to Gridley Memorial Hospital, which was only ten minutes away with Richard driving.

He took me to the emergency room, and I was not surprised to learn that something was wrong. An x-ray revealed that I had a broken collarbone. The doctor told me that if the collarbone broke the other way, it would have cut a major artery.

Later that night, Mr. Andreason came to my house to make sure that I was okay. He said that Mr. Nelson was very sorry. Mr. Nelson claimed that he had no idea that I was really hurt. The principal also told me that Mr. Nelson would be transferring to another school.

I stayed home for a week to let my collarbone heal. I was lucky that it healed quickly. Within a month, I was close to being normal again.

CHAPTER 4

My cousin Kenny worked a full-time job on a paper route eight hours at night during his junior and senior years. That was why he was able to purchase a 1964 Malibu 327 SS Super Sport convertible. It was a "chick magnet."

Even though he received a lot of attention in the car, he had only owned it a short time when he decided to sell it. I was able to buy it on time with payments through Bank of America in Live Oak. Wow, my car a Malibu convertible!

Kenny bought a special-made dune buggy sure to catch even more attention. He had to wait a full month for it to be built. It was made from a Volkswagen frame, an all-fiberglass body, an open roof, chrome wheels, metallic blue, and drop-dead gorgeous.

The funny part was that Kenny had been told that the dune buggy could double as a boat. When he told me this, I said, "I don't believe it."

Kenny said, "It's true, and I'll prove it. We'll go to the Feather River between Yuba City and Marysville and drive across it on Saturday."

Kenny was so excited to try it. I couldn't talk him out of it. So, on Saturday, we chose a spot on the Feather River, where it was deep enough to prove Kenny's theory.

Kenny was so confidant as we drove into the river. The deeper into the water we got, the faster it sank! Water was pouring in through the windows. We had to swim to shore as we watched his new dune buggy sink and go down with the current.

By the time we walked back to town and found some help to tow the car from the river, the swift water and rocks had done too much damage. Kenny had to buy a new car.

This time, he bought a family-type car so that he could work his paper route at night. It was a Chevrolet Impala and nothing fancy. I think he was always sorry that he sold his Malibu convertible to me.

Chapter 5

We only lived about a two-hour drive from Reno, Nevada, so Kenny, Richard, and I would drive up, play some slots, drink beer, and get thrown out for being underage. I couldn't understand why a person my age could go to Vietnam and die for their country but could not buy a beer in the States.

It didn't take long for me to find a solution to the age problem. Being excellent on a typewriter and using erasing tape and new lamination, I changed the date of birth on my California driver's license, making me officially twenty-one. It wasn't great, as the typing did not match up exactly, but it did work. I also changed Kenny's driver's license. His turned out even better than mine. I also changed Richard's. His worked well until he handed it to a grocer (Sunny Behr) at Sunny's Market in Live Oak, who actually knew him. The grocer wouldn't give it back. Richard had to go to DMV and get a new driver's license.

First period at school was when the office made announcements. Usually, these were insignificant titbits. Near the end of my senior year, during one of these announcements, we were all devastated to hear that another classmate's older brother, Darrel Wheeler, had been killed in Vietnam. I had been a friend of his younger brother, Gordon, since grade school.

Our classroom was suddenly a buzz of alarm. Gordon was not at school. Everyone needed to talk at once. It was shocking to have the brutal war images we saw each night on the TV news affecting Live Oak so personally. The whole town was saddened and upset. I did not understand why American boys were there in the first place. Suddenly, the war was very real and threatening.

Although our principal, Mr. Andreason, was able to calm us, as soon as the bell rang, we hit the hallway, and the discussions resumed. Some classmates close to the Wheeler family filled in the details for the rest of us. We were so upset that when the second-period bell rang, many students were late to class.

We found out later that forty-eight Americans had been killed in the fight that cost Darrel his life.

That night, I called Kenny, and a small group of us made a plan to cut school and meet at the river bottom to talk about what had happened.

The next day, I rode with Richard. Kenny was already there when we arrived at the river. Another classmate, Larry Miles, and another friend of his were there as well. Kenny focused on how far he could throw and how many skims he got from one of the hundreds of rocks along the river's edge. We each joined in, a total of five, all throwing rocks. Kenny won the competition with six skims.

While competing for distance and skims, we tried to make sense of the mess the adults had left for us in the world. Our lives were just beginning, and it seemed that others before us had created unnecessary problems and wars. Each of us imagined a happy future of reaching our dreams and enjoying life.

It was during this disappointing discussion that we heard tires crunching on the dirt road beyond the small trees and large bushes lining the riverbank. We scattered into the vegetation to spy on who had arrived.

"Police!" hissed Richard. He motioned us to follow him through the trees and bushes back to his car tucked further down the road, hidden from sight.

A policeman entered the clearing right where Kenny and I were standing. Knowing the others would have made it to the car, we tried to bluff.

"Hello, boys. What are you doing out here?"

Quickly, without thinking, I answered, "Fishing."

He sort of laughed. I realized it sounded lame because we had no poles and no tackle box. But I couldn't think of anything better. In the distance, we heard Richard start up his car. Richard made it. He drove off.

"Okay, boys. I'll take you back to school," said the sheriff.

He drove Kenny to his high school in Marysville, about a twenty-minute drive. Then, he delivered me back to Live Oak High School, in the patrol car. Kenny and I smiled at each other in the backseat behind the metal grate of the patrol car. We chuckled, finding this criminal treatment amusing. It would make a great story at the next river party.

"Can you turn on the siren when we get out on the highway?" asked Kenny. This idea set us off giggling for most of the ride.

"This is not a joke," was the sheriff's reply. "You are both in big trouble, and your schools will not take this lightly."

Since it was my first time getting caught cutting school, I only received a one-week suspension. Mr. Andreason was very good with me but stern. He told me if I wanted to graduate never to cut school again.

Mom wasn't happy about the suspension, but Dad thought it was good so that we could go fishing for the week. Dad was known to close his jewelry store at times to go hunting or fishing. We camped for five days up by Quincy in the High Sierras, catching native brook trout and German browns. In the afternoon, we would also target practice. Dad was an excellent shot. We would practice with pistols, and at least one or two deer rifles. What a fun week!

Kenny was not so lucky. He had been caught before and put on probation. This time, his school suspended him for the rest of the year. That meant Kenny could not graduate in two months with the rest of his class. His mom was very upset. Kenny had been forging her name on notes all year.

The probation made Kenny consider joining the army and getting his GED (General Educational Development Certificate) through the military.

His father, Lloyd Denney, was a POW in WWII and lived on only one cup of water and one piece of bread a day for eleven months in captivity. Initially, Lloyd had been a gunner on tanks until he was thrown off and broke both of his elbows. After healing, he became the company cook until they were captured. During this time, my aunt Nora thought he was gone for good. When the war ended and he was rescued, he had lost over fifty pounds.

Uncle Lloyd would talk to Kenny a lot about the army and the war. Kenny had grown up in a very pro-military family, so naturally, he would consider joining the army.

The next couple of months passed quickly. We had several late-night parties at the river or the drive-in, all ending the same way, all of us wondering what to do after graduation.

I did have a distant cousin Cliff Caffall stop by for a visit. He had just returned from Vietnam. He visited with my parents for a while then he took me for a ride. We drove around the Sutter Buttes, the smallest mountain range in the world, but still close to home. Cliff started talking about Vietnam and I was listening. He was Para Rescue in the Air Force. He was constantly flown into battle to bring out the wounded by chopper. His stories could easily bring tears as he had so many guys die in his arms! Cliff was on his way to Alaska for a new duty station and who knows from there. I wondered later if I will ever see him again?

When graduation finally arrived, Kenny sat with Mom and Dad to watch the ceremony when I graduated.

After the ceremony, Mr. Andreason actually walked up and talked to me. He said I should sign up for college right away or take the chance of being drafted. I felt so good that he came over to talk to me. (Maybe I should have taken his advice.)

CHAPTER 6

THE YEAR WAS 1968, when I graduated. I was seventeen years old. It marked a significant change in my life in far greater ways than no longer being a student. North Korea captured the USS *Pueblo* in January, Martin Luther King was assassinated in April, Robert F. Kennedy was assassinated in June, and Richard Nixon was running for president. Life as I had known it was about to take a horrible turn, as it would for so many others.

The summer following graduation was full of decisions. Should I go to college and wait to be drafted or join now and get it over with? If I joined the army, it would be one way to see the world, and I was ready to see the world.

Live Oak does get a little small.

In August, I received a letter from one of my class friends, Larry Miles, who joined the army right after graduation. Larry enjoyed coming to our river parties or the drive-in. He used to drink a bit and reminisce about his girlfriend, Kathy, dying of cancer at age fourteen. She was so beautiful, and Larry was just devastated. Larry was raised by a single mom and had to be the man of the family at a very young age.

At age fifteen, Larry walked into the house and caught his stepdad beating his mom. Larry, being much smaller, grabbed a cane in the living room that was left there by an uncle. He beat his stepdad so badly that he had to go to the hospital.

At age sixteen, Larry received the call from his grandfather that the stepdad had just attacked Larry's mom for the last time. As the stepdad broke down the front door, the grandfather shot him four times with his .22 rifle. He did survive but was never the same. He had to move out of state and live with other relatives to help him. Larry's mom filed for divorce, and no one ever saw his stepfather again.

Larry seemed to like the army, even though he said the training was rough. He was on his way to his new duty station in Alaska. How exciting. He was getting to travel and see new places. So far, in my life, I had only been to the states of Nevada and Oregon. I had a desire to travel and see the world.

CHAPTER 7

WELL, IT FINALLY happened. Kenny and I decided to join the army on the Buddy System. That meant we would stay together throughout basic training and maybe the next training school as well. We decided this late one night at a party, and then woke up our parents in the middle of the night to spring the news. My parents did not want me to go. They wanted me to stay and go to Yuba College, but they agreed to sign for me. I did not turn eighteen for another month. Kenny's parents thought it was a good idea for him, and he could get his GED.

The following day, we all met at the recruiter's office and discussed what we could do in the army. Kenny wanted to go wherever we would be needed. The recruiter convinced us to let our training guide us. He said that after testing from the army, they would know what would be the best jobs for both of us. After signing papers, we were given an allowance for the bus trip to Oakland, CA, to the Induction Center for testing and a physical. I was now getting scared. This was becoming *too* real. It was one thing to talk about, but actually doing it was scary! Not only was this going to change my life, but it could also *end* my life.

Goodbyes were not easy. I was leaving several girlfriends and a childhood that most people only wished they had.

As I left for the bus, my father said to my mother, "Look at your little boy. This will be the last time you ever see him. When he returns, he will be a man." We were all crying, and it was a very sad goodbye.

Upon our arrival into Oakland, we were put up in a cheap hotel room across the street from the Induction Center. That night at the hotel bar, we learned that life in the big city was quite different from Live Oak. They had what was called "Dime a Dance." The guys would buy coupons worth ten cents each and give a girl a coupon for a dance. One thing about it, you never have to worry about getting turned down. I bought one dollar's worth and waited for the slow songs.

I had to be conservative with my money because the army was only going to pay me eighty-four dollars per month as a Private E1. In fact, my car payment was one hundred and thirty dollars per month, but luckily, my parents were going to help me. My father said he would even drive my car occasionally to keep it up.

After leaving the bar, we went next door for even more of a shock. Strippers—yes, these girls took off *all* their clothes during the dance. The song "Summertime" will never be the same! Actually, it was very embarrassing but fun, and both Kenny and I had to act cool in front of all the other guys. The entire room was filled with guys facing the induction in the morning. Wow, what a night to remember.

The next morning, we walked over to the Induction Center, where we were herded around like cattle for tests and physical exams. All the men were being herded around in their underwear. They did not consider us humans, and they let you know it. The written tests were simple, and both Kenny and I did so well that we were offered Officer Candidate School if we would stay in the army for six years.

Both of us declined the offer.

This was starting to sound more like a prison sentence, and when I looked around, it also looked like one. I was having second thoughts about what I was doing. Being herded around this huge building in just my underwear was quite embarrassing. They poked, prodded, and squeezed us—all kinds of medical and physical tests in one day. I was worried about the vision test because of my lazy eye, which I'd had since a baby, but I passed OK.

Now, it was time for the hearing test. I was given a headset and told to push the button when I heard the tone. I didn't know my hearing was bad, but I never heard the sound. They tested the equipment, and it was fine.

A uniformed clerk handed back my papers. "Sorry, you can't join with hearing like that."

Well, this was my big chance. I tried to enlist and couldn't. I had a great excuse to return home now and still not lose face.

Kenny said, "No way! I am not going in without you. We're on the Buddy System."

He took my papers and got back in line for the hearing test. He stated his name as mine. After he passed the hearing test for me, we were all herded into a large room. In unison, all the recruits said the oath, and we were officially in the army.

Yikes!

We were all given an allowance and orders to report to our basic training schools. Kenny and I are going to Fort Lewis, Washington.

CHAPTER 8

THAT AFTERNOON, WE boarded our plane and flew up to Fort Lewis. The plane was full of guys starting basic training the next day. Most of the guys on the flight were drafted and not happy at all. Very few like us had enlisted, and we were actually looked down on. This was not a time that you admitted to joining.

We took a bus to Travis Air Base and boarded the airplane. It was a military airplane with no windows. The airplane ride was fun for me as it was my first time.

Parts of Ft. Lewis looked beautiful and green, and other parts looked like typical, dull, old military barracks. It was dark by the time we reached our units. We were rushed into a barracks, given a bunk, and told to go to bed. We would be getting up very early the next morning. I ended up on a top bunk and Kenny on the bottom.

All of a sudden, a light came on, and a man in uniform appeared wearing a Smokey the Bear-type hat. He was yelling at us as loud as he could and started punching the cigarette butt cans that were located beside each bunk with his fists. Terrified? Oh yes! He was telling us we were the worst looking bunch of recruits he had ever seen, and it was his job to make men out of us in only eight weeks. This was Sergeant White, our "DI" (drill instructor), a Black man about six feet tall and as mean as they come. Sgt. White had spent two tours in Vietnam and held two black belts in martial arts.

On our first day, we had "all" of our hair cut off, issued military uniforms, and ran everywhere . . . just to wait in line when you got there.

Hurry up and wait.

Unless the drill sergeant had you doing push-ups while you were waiting in line. Push-ups were not easy to do when he put his foot on your back to weigh you down. He also counted for you and would get hung up on one number like 15, 15, 15, 15, 16, 16, etc.

We were allowed three minutes each in the chow hall, which was just enough time to sit down, inhale your food, and drink your coffee on the way to the door. And, yes, guess who was waiting at the door. It was him.

"Run, run, run."

I can't understand how anyone could yell so much. He literally screamed at us all day long. He was not picking on me in particular. He hated *all* of us. That night, he ran us back to our barracks and said if any of us did not like him that he would enjoy a good fight right then and there. He said, "Come one, come all."

Standing there with his fists doubled up and jumping around like a boxer, he *really* wanted to hit somebody.

Well, nobody said a word.

He cussed and messed with our heads. "You are just a bunch of sissies. Also, don't forget 'Jody' back home, the one without the balls to enlist. Well, guess what? He's screwing your girl right now, and there's *nothing* you can do about it."

After he finally got tired of yelling insults, he ordered, "Go to bed and don't say a word because I'm getting you up early tomorrow morning to *really* start training."

I thought I knew all of the cuss words, but I was learning some new ones.

At my bunk, I was so tired I could hardly lift myself onto the top bunk. It was very quiet after the lights went out with only a few whispers like, "Oh shit!"

I was wondering now . . . What did I do?

All of a sudden, the lights came on. It was him, yelling as loud as he could, saying we had ten minutes to shower and shave, or we would get an extra twenty push-ups before breakfast. In ten minutes, we were all standing at attention for his inspection.

He did find one guy that did not shave, and because of him, we all got an extra twenty push-ups before we began our day. His name was Ned from Arkansas. A nice guy but very slow, mentally. His slow accent didn't help, either. As we were all doing our push-ups, I heard a few murmurs to him, saying, " You've had it."

Twenty correct push-ups are a lot of push-ups for anyone. Many guys think they can do twenty correct push-ups, but it is not as easy as it sounds, especially with the drill instructors "help." Some guys were lying on their stomachs after about fifteen, but with this drill instructor yelling at the top of his voice, it kept you going. After the last one finally finished, we did get to go eat, and of course, we only had three minutes.

With only three minutes to eat, you would think that the guys would try to work together. No. There was always a practical joker that would loosen the top of the saltshaker so that when you poured it, salt would pour out so heavy that you could not even eat the food. Or you reached for a clean coffee cup and found a cigarette butt in it.

Oh well, you learn to live with it as you have nobody to complain to except the other guys in the unit, and they are all going through the same thing.

After breakfast, in formation, Sgt. White called "attention" and told us what a delightful day we were going to have. We would be running everywhere, taking in a few forty-minute classes, which turned out to be the only breaks we would get, with push-ups, pull-ups, sit-ups, and cussed at all day. By nightfall, we were all exhausted and hurt all over. Kenny thought he was going to die, and I thought I was close.

I knew now that I had made a Big Mistake by joining the army!

As soon as the light went out, I heard someone screaming. It sounded like he was taking a real beating. I jumped out of my bunk, only to land on Kenny getting out of his bunk. We fell in the dark, got up, and ran to the other end. We found Ned, the kid who didn't shave, lying on the floor beaten up. We helped him up and back onto his bunk. He had a bloody nose but seemed OK.

Morning came too soon. Sergeant White was yelling again, saying that we overslept, and he wanted us up *and* showered by 4:00 a.m., not up *at* 4:00 a.m. It was tough to get up because I hurt all over. When Sgt. White saw the guy who got beat up, he smiled and said: "I bet you shave every day from now on . . . ha-ha."

Well, this day was as bad as the day before, but now we had started a new game Sergeant White liked. When anyone made a mistake, he would carry a rock with him until someone made another mistake, and then he would carry a bigger rock. You had to carry your rock to the chow hall, to the bathroom, in the shower, and to bed. Do not let the DI ever catch you without your rock, and whatever you do, do not let it get dirty or set it on the ground. This rock started out to be the size of a baseball but seemed to be getting bigger by the minute. The DI said his last bunch of sissies had to carry a rock so big at the end that it took two of them to carry it.

Sgt. White chose a squad leader among us to be his ears at night, to make sure we were all up, showered, shaved, and standing at attention for his inspection at 4:00 a.m. Terry was chosen to be the new squad leader, a real kiss ass. Terry was a little white prick that nobody liked. He was about five foot ten and 180 pounds. He thought he was better than the rest of us. He was from the East Coast and had the attitude to prove it.

Sgt. White also told us that we have no race or color in the Army, as we are all Green. He says, "by the time we get to Vietnam we must all fight together like we are brothers."

The night went by fast—too fast.

Sgt. White woke us up again, yelling as usual. He told Terry he should start getting us up by 3:00 a.m. He claimed that one of the officers saw us yesterday and said that we were the worst looking bunch of recruits he had ever seen, and it was his job to get us in shape. So now, we were going to have to work much harder and longer. We were going to start the day with a sixteen-mile run, and if anyone fell Sgt. White would kick him until he got up.

I was good at running, but sixteen miles was a long way for anyone, especially if you were carrying "the rock." Luckily, I did not have it. Only one guy fell, but he was up and running before the DI could kick him. Sgt. White was truly in excellent shape. He did not even breathe hard after sixteen miles and kept yelling all the way, telling those who were about to drop to go ahead and drop so he could kick their ass. It was a great incentive to keep us moving.

Another time, one guy fell out, and a Native American Indian that we all called "Chief" had him grab onto his pack and literally dragged him the rest of the way. It was not unusual when a recruit fell for the entire platoon to run another 100 yards, then 100 yards back to get the private who fell. Believe me, the entire company was not your friends if you were the person who fell out during the run, as they had to run another 200 yards because you fell out. I quickly learned how to "call cadence." We had to be the loudest unit, calling cadence when passing another unit, or Sergeant White would punish us. He said that we could never be second place, or he would make us pay dearly. With that incentive, we learned to really scream loud. When calling cadence, you will follow whatever the DI is calling, such as:

You had *a good home, but now you have left-your right*
And Jody was there waiting when you left-your right
And your girl was there when you left-your right
But Jody took your girl when you left-your right

Sound off, 1–2
Sound off, 1–2
Sound off, 1–2–3–4, sound off!

After our run that day, we were photographed, fingerprinted, and issued military ID cards. We were told no one could alter these laminated cards. At that time, I could see through the corner of my eye that Kenny was smiling at me, knowing that I would change my birth date on this card as soon as I got to a typewriter. If I was able to change the California driver's license, I would certainly be able to change a military ID card.

We couldn't control ourselves. We both broke out laughing. Sgt. White quickly wiped the smiles off our faces, demanding we give him twenty push-ups. He yelled and cussed at us all the way through it. At least he didn't make the other guys do push-ups, or they would have been after us. We finally finished our push-ups with the help of Sergeant White's "incentive" that, if we collapsed, he would kick us.

CHAPTER 9

WE HAD NOW been in basic for one week. Even Kenny thought we made a mistake. College would have been much easier. But it was a little late now. So, we were going to have to make the best of it. Kenny was dying for a beer. He was sure there must be a way to get a brew. Basic training is eight weeks long, and Kenny said he couldn't make it eight weeks without a brew. I had to laugh to myself, thinking that nobody enjoys a cold beer more than Kenny.

Sgt. White enjoyed fighting and had us all slap fight each other throughout the day. He taught us how to block the incoming blows and strike back with an open hand. If you hit anyone with a closed fist, Sergeant White would jump in with multiple kicks to end the fight. He also taught us how to kick and when to kick. I think he liked to kick as much as he liked to hit. My dad's lessons in boxing helped me so much, especially in blocking incoming blows.

As the days went on, we heard that if you could sneak out at night over to the Advanced Infantry side of the base, you could drink 3.2 beer in the Enlisted Men's Club (EM Club), and we would blend in like AIT (Advanced Infantry Training) students. Kenny thought it worth trying, but if we got caught, we'd get it. In fact, *all* of us would be punished. Was it really worth it? Kenny thought so.

In the next couple of days, we found out from the cooks in the mess hall how to get over to the AIT side. They laughed at us when I said that we wanted to go.

Kenny finally talked me into it.

We were going. Everyone else was asleep except us. We sneaked out past Terry, the squad leader, as we didn't want him to rat on us. We went out onto the street and hid under the darkness of telephone poles. It took us about an hour of sneaking and hiding to make our way to the other side of the base to the Enlisted Men's Club. Our adrenalin was running. How exciting. We made it. Now, we would enjoy a few beers and make our way back to the basic camp.

The club was noisy. Lots of guys were drinking and talking. It was easy to blend in when we are all dressed the same. The only problem that I could see was that our uniforms did not show a rank insignia. But nobody seemed to notice it. About midnight, we started our sneak walk back to the basic training side of the base. We did it, and sneaking past Terry wasn't easy with a buzz, as we couldn't stop giggling.

The next day was horrible as we drank too much 3.2 beer at the EM Club. Kenny said that he felt about half sick.

Today, above and beyond all the exercises and running we were going to do, we also had to crawl under barbed wire with live fire above us. That meant there would be real bullets eight inches above us, and we were both hungover. I now realize why they would not allow you to drink during basic training.

A few of the guys now heard that we snuck out for beers, and they wanted to go with us the next time.

We had now made it through our first two weeks somehow. Small groups of friends had formed, and a few fights had broken out at night. Our group of friends was talking about our first paycheck. Some of us were planning a poker game after dark. Of course, this would all be hidden from Terry, as he was such a fink that he would tell Sergeant White immediately.

The next couple of weeks were as bad as the first. Work out all day, run all day, slap fight all day. Each day, Sgt. White pushed us harder to the point that you thought you were not going to make it.

A day at the firing range was like a day off, as I always enjoyed shooting. Kenny scored higher than I did in marksmanship. He had excellent eyesight. Me, I always had trouble focusing with my lazy eye.

By now, I could look around and see a few who would not make it. These guys would be recycled once before being discharged. That meant after eight weeks of basic, they would not graduate and would have to start all over again. I could not imagine it.

Our company also lost two recruits to spinal meningitis.

We had now been issued M14 rifles and about fifty pounds of gear to carry on our backs wherever we go. I enjoyed shooting the M14. It sort of reminded me of my dad's 30-06 deer rifle. I did wonder why we were training with the M14 when, in Vietnam, they were using the M16, a lighter and faster shooting rifle.

"The Rock" was getting much larger. We were only four weeks into basic, and it was already the size of a football. Both Kenny and I had had it a couple of times, but not since it had become so large. This was no longer funny. One thing about it, you usually only carried it a few hours before someone else goofed up. And at least I had not had to sleep with it.

I really thought after a while that the soreness would eventually go away, but each day, it was just as hard to get up as the last, except now, the squad leader, Terry, yelled at us every morning to get us going. I think he learned this from Sgt. White.

It was finally payday. A full month is a long stretch between pay-days, but we did not have anywhere to spend it anyway except the few nights that we snuck over to the other side of the base to drink 3.2 beers. Now, four of us sneak over to the AIT side of the base. I learned quickly only to drink a couple of beers, even though they were only 3.2

percent alcohol. Most normal beers are at least 4 to 5 percent.

My paycheck was pretty sad . . . eighty-four dollars per month as a Private E1. I made more money working at the gas station after school.

That night was our poker game. Even as tired as we were from the day, we could still stay up most of the night and play poker. At least Terry approved of poker, as long as we kept it a secret from Sgt. White. Terry did lay down most of his check during the night, but eighty-four dollars did not last very long. I could see that these poker games would only be about one night a month as nobody would have any money at all in a couple of days. Most of the married men could not play because they had to send money home to their wives.

Each morning and throughout the day in every class, each instructor would tell you how your wife or girlfriend is sleeping with "Jody." Jody was your best friend, brother, neighbor, etc., who was sleeping with your girl and enjoying your eighty-four dollars. You could see the blood vessels bulging on the faces of the married guys, as the instructor would say: "Remember how firm your girl's breasts feel? Well, Jody is sucking on one right now. Also, your baby will never call you daddy again, because Jody is now daddy!" This never bothered me, but the married guys were about ready to kill their best friends or brothers.

Our slap fights were becoming much more aggressive. Sgt. White now had us all kicking each other throughout the matches. He had taught us sidekicks to the knees and straight kicks to the crotch. When a kick landed between the legs, it usually ended the fight. Unless, of course, Sergeant White decided to kick the loser one more time for losing.

We had now lost several men to the hospital over these kicks. Raymond had been taken to the hospital twice. Raymond was about five foot ten and weighed about 200 pounds with no muscle. He was not real bright and the weakest guy in our unit. Kenny told Raymond not to take these beatings, just fall to the ground once you're hit and act like you're in a lot of pain. The most that would happen to you was that Sergeant White would kick you one last time.

After four weeks of basic, the married guys were allowed to have their wives come on base and spend the night. They were taken to another part of the base. This was like having a day off, but you had to have a wife to get the day off. We were all so jealous! These guys got a room and a girl. How great is that?

For those of us that did not have a wife to spend the day off with, Sergeant White promised to fill our day. As he put it, "If all of us had wives, we would all have a day off," including him. But because we are not good enough to have a wife, he was stuck with us. Now, he was going to make *us* pay.

We started with a ten-mile run. Raymond fell after only a few miles. Sgt. White kicked him so hard I did not think he would get off the ground at all, but he did. He was crying, trying to run, limping along with Sergeant White right behind him, waiting for him to fall again. I thought to myself if Raymond falls and Sergeant White kicks him again, I would step in, but I knew I could not win against Sergeant White. Luckily, Raymond did not fall again. I tried to talk with him later, but he was crying like a little girl.

After our run, we spent the rest of the day practicing hand-to-hand combat with Sgt. White. I thought this might be a good chance to get in a good blow as I was chosen for the demonstration. He was teaching us how to take a man's legs out from under him by kicking him in the knee, and how to counter it. I had the opportunity of trying to kick Sgt. White's legs out from under him while trying to land a blow on his nose. As it turned out, when I tried kicking him, he kicked me between my legs so hard I thought I would never walk again. When I fell to the ground, he said, "This kick always works" and yelled, "Get up," as he chose another participant. I could hardly get up but had no choice. By the time I got off the ground, another guy was down. Sgt. White was going through these guys one after another, and we could tell he was really enjoying himself. Then I realized my nose was bleeding. He must have also hit me in the face, and I didn't feel it with all of the pain going on below. I looked around, and all of the guys coming off the ground looked like they had taken a real beating.

Sgt. White *loved* beating people. And he was right on color, he was not particular at all, he just enjoyed beating on all of us!

I didn't know how he could even stand himself.

That night, we dragged ourselves back to our barracks. The married guys met us. They were coming back from their "day with the wives." Some had big smiles, while others were cussing how they were going to kill Jody! None of them got any sympathy from us after what we had been through.

The next day proved interesting, watching Sergeant White beat on all of the married guys, and *we* got to stand back and watch. One guy, in particular, made a big mistake. He tried to have an all-out fistfight with Sergeant White.

Jimmy from the Bronx thought he was so tough. He was six foot and 180 lbs. Sergeant White kicked him at least three times in a row between the legs, and Jimmy never landed a blow. This guy was turning blue, and he could not get off the ground. Sergeant White bent down to help him off the ground and said, "You have spunk, kid, but you need to learn how to fight. Now, walk on your own two feet."

He could hardly walk, but did, knowing he had no choice. He was bleeding around the nose and mouth, so it was obvious he took a few blows to the face, but Sergeant White was so fast you could not see his moves.

At the end of his training class, Sergeant White told the married guys that this special training session was to make us all equal, meaning now, he had been able to beat on all of us.

As we returned to our barracks, Sergeant White said, "Sweet dreams, and remember, that's not you in your girl's bed. It's Jody," and walked off.

CHAPTER 10

FIGHTS WERE BREAKING out every night. The rock was now much larger than a football. One guy was really complaining about having to take the rock with him to see his wife. He said it was most embarrassing in bed.

Kenny and I were sneaking out a couple of times a week over to the AIT side at night for a few beers. The poker games died down a few days after payday because most of us were broke. Only one guy came out a big winner, "Snyder," from Chicago, who claimed he had never lost. Snyder, a white guy with a big mouth, had a small frame but was very good with a knife. He enjoyed practicing his knife throws every night in the barracks, and no big guys ever picked on him.

We would be getting paid again at the end of basic, so there would be one more opportunity to meet Snyder with a deck of cards, and he had several people waiting, including me.

Sergeant White was laughing the following morning. The man never laughed, so something was up. He said today we would all be getting our shots and warned us not to cry like babies, as it was nothing compared to the shots we would be getting for Vietnam.

I could not believe it. I was in a line of about 100 guys, with our shirts off and a row of medics on both sides. They were giving us shots with needle guns in both arms so fast they were ripping the skin. This really hurt, and there were tears in many eyes. But, at the end was a big smile . . . Sergeant White said, "Girls, let's go to work, and none of you better get sick on me today with these shots, or I will make *all* of you pay for it."

Throughout the day, several guys had reactions to the shots, including Kenny, who was turning green. Sergeant White chose a nice, large rock for Kenny and told him, "Run with this rock around this pole until the green leaves you." Kenny looked terrible, running around the pole carrying that big rock as sick as one could be.

After a few minutes, I could not help it. I burst out laughing.

I knew I was in trouble, but I could not hold back. Kenny looked horrible. Then, my laugh ended suddenly when Sergeant White told Kenny to stop running and chose a nice big rock for me.

This rock was not funny.

Now, I was carrying an M14 rifle, about fifty pounds on my back, *and* a twenty-pound rock. Sergeant White thought it would be a good idea if I ran around the pole for Kenny. Luckily, there was not enough time because we had a class starting.

Kenny was beginning to look better now that he was not running around that pole.

We had many classes throughout the day, in between exercises and running. We had map classes (how to read a map and grid), survival classes, live bayonet training, hand-to-hand training, hand grenades, claymore mines, exercises, and lots of practice with the M14 at pop-up targets.

That day's session was on hand-to-hand. I thought, "OH NO, it's just another excuse for Sergeant White to beat on us," but there was another instructor. This instructor taught us how to use a bayonet during hand-to-hand. We were using real bayonets, but nobody got hurt during this drill. As for the knife, he said if, for some reason, you have no weapon and someone pulls a big knife on you (probably more in a bar fight than in a war situation), you pivot on one foot to about-face and run like hell.

Sergeant White did not like this.

He asked the other instructor to pull a knife on him, and he would show us how to make the other guy eat it. I really wanted to see this, but the other instructor wanted no part of Sergeant White, not even with a knife to defend himself.

Well, class was over, and I was still packing this big rock. I could not believe nobody goofed up during the class. Now, it was very serious; *nobody* wanted the rock.

We ran back to the chow hall for lunch. We had three minutes, of course, and I had to balance my tray on the rock. Today's lunch was SOS (Shit on a Shingle), and the shingle was the cold toast that didn't get eaten in the morning. It was so bad I thought I would cover it in salt and pepper, and when I went to salt it, the top came off, and salt poured all over my shingle. I couldn't believe that I fell for this. I could hardly eat my shingle.

After lunch, one of the guys vomited. When I saw that, I almost lost my lunch as well, but I didn't have enough inside me to lose. Sergeant White had this guy clean up the vomit from the ground while he chose a nice big rock for him. He told me to put my rock on the ground gently. As I did, he said, "Don't look so relieved. You'll be carrying it again."

This kid was really sick. Now, he was standing there with dry heaves while holding this big rock. Sergeant White kept yelling at him not to vomit anymore on his ground. Finally, Sergeant White told him he better run over to the medics, " but if they don't put you in the hospital, you better have your ass back here within a half hour with my rock." The guy never did come back. I heard he was hospitalized with yellow jaundice.

Sergeant White told us that he would choose another big rock and issue it to someone in the morning. I hoped it was not me.

Morning came too soon, and there he was, yelling at us again. This time, he decided to give the rock to Terry, our squad leader, for kissing his ass so much. Sergeant White told Terry that he had never seen anyone kiss ass like him. He said to Terry, "Your lips must hurt." I thought that I was going to lose it. We were all standing at attention, and I know everyone must have been holding back a big grin but dare not show it. It was all I could do to refrain from laughing. Nobody liked Terry. He was nothing but a big kiss ass. Then it became even funnier when I realized that all of us at attention were dying with laughter inside but frozen on the outside.

Everyone worked extra hard that day to ensure that Terry would be stuck with the rock all day and hopefully have to sleep with it as well. The rock was getting so large it was difficult to run with it. Yes, Terry kept the rock all day and night. But that night, he kept us up until midnight polishing the floor. He was punishing us because he had to carry the rock. I guess this is what you call the "chain of command."

CHAPTER 11

THE NEXT MORNING was hand grenade training. It did not take long for someone else to carry the rock. Sergeant White explained that throwing a hand grenade can be very dangerous, and his rock would sit on the ground for this training. It had happened in the past that some guy that was not very bright had blown himself up. We lined up with live hand grenades, were shown how to hold the grenade, pull the pin, count, and throw. I got as far away from Raymond and a couple of others as possible in case they blew themselves up. Everyone in our class learned to toss the grenade properly, even Raymond.

We only had a couple more weeks, and the soreness had finally stopped, and I had never before felt so strong. Several of the guys had decided to kick Sergeant White's ass before we graduated. He still claimed that we all looked like a bunch of girls and that he should recycle all of us, but he was tired of looking at us and wanted a group of real men to work with.

Terry got his ass beat last night. Nobody claims to have heard a thing. Someone threw a blanket over his head while he was sleeping, and several guys worked him over. Of course, he reported this to Sergeant White. Sergeant White decided that Terry should carry the rock for not winning the fight and gave him an extra twenty-five push-ups to strengthen his arms while all of us watched. Terry was pretty strong, but he could hardly do the push-ups after taking such a beating. When he stood up, he looked terrible. Both eyes were swollen, black and blue, and his nose was bleeding again.

When Sergeant White handed him this huge rock, I couldn't stand it. I broke out laughing. I tried to hold it back, but it was too late. Sergeant White caught me. He said, "Travis, I told you that you would carry the rock again." When he handed me the rock, Kenny broke out laughing. Sergeant White told me to hand the rock over to Kenny to wipe the grin off of his face. It worked. Kenny was no longer grinning. This rock was getting so big that you could hardly carry it. Off we went running to another class with Kenny packing the rock. I wanted to laugh badly now, but as long as I didn't look over at Kenny, I could hold it back.

In this class, we would discuss where we would be going for more training after basic. Most guys were drafted, so their service number had a US preceding the number. If you joined, you had an RA before the number. We only had a few RA guys who had chosen schools of interest, such as mechanics, aviation, etc. Kenny and I would be going on for more specialized combat, pre-airborne training.

We were told the worst place you could go to is a place called Camp Crockett in Georgia. Some students died in that training. I thought to myself, with all of the different places to go, we certainly would not get stuck in Camp Crockett. Orders would not be cut until our last day, so we wouldn't know where we were going until graduation, but no matter where we went, we would get a full month (thirty-day leave) prior to our next training school. I could hardly wait.

That night, all thoughts were on the future, where we would go, and the past . . . the wonderful life that I had left behind.

Sergeant White assured us that many of us would die in Vietnam. He said, "Charlie (the Viet Cong) is just waiting for you to get out of your training."

CHAPTER 12

WITH THE UNCERTAINTY and apprehension of what was to come, my mind started drifting to my home and girlfriends I had left behind, like Joy, from Gridley, whom I dated throughout high school. Joy was a petite blonde with hair down to her waist. She was the bishop's daughter of the Mormon Church, and I considered her the marrying type. Her parents were very strict. We had to wait until she turned sixteen to go on a date. She knew I was on the wild side, playing the guitar, singing at beach parties, and seeing other girls. I did take Joy to the junior prom at Live Oak High. She looked so gorgeous that night.

Cheryl also knew I was dating other girls, but she warned me to stop, or she would start seeing other guys, and finally did. We dated throughout my senior year, and I took her to the senior prom.

Peggy, from Yuba City, whom I dated throughout high school, was an attractive, five foot six blonde and always cheated on me. I knew she was sneaking out with other guys, but, hey, I would sneak out with one of my other girls. We had a good "understanding."

I'd dated Gerri from Sutter just before I entered the army. We dated for about two months and were becoming very close before I left.

Two Live Oak girls, Sharon and Virginia, were considered good friends, and they did go out with Kenny and I. Both loved to party at the river or go with us to the drive-in, where Richard, Kenny, and I would all row up our cars together. We called them the "good girls." They would go out with us and party but "no touching."

My mind even drifted to my very first girlfriend, Karen, in first grade. We would walk to her house after school and watch TV until my mom would pick me up after work. One day, we walked to my dad's jewelry store downtown. Karen liked one of the rings in the window, so I gave it to her. That night, her mom called my mom and said that Karen had a "real" diamond ring.

Mom told me that Dad would talk to me when he got home. I knew I was in big trouble.

Later that night, after Dad got home, he explained to me why I couldn't just give things away like that out of the store. He wasn't mad as Karen's mom returned the ring the next day anyway. Dad told me this just shows that I am "a chip off of the old block." By the second and third grade, I would lose Karen, as she was getting so cute, all of the boys were after her. Karen would become one of the most popular girls in school.

Then my mind drifted back to reality.

What had I done? I was starting to realize that I had really screwed up. How could I have ever left that life for this one? I thought of my loving parents, how they did not want me to go. I finally drifted off to sleep in tears.

The next couple of weeks went by rather fast. All of us had changed a lot in the past eight weeks. I don't think I had a day off except for KP duty (kitchen patrol). You either peel potatoes, or wash dishes and clean all day—a full twelve-hour shift. It was still easier than a workout with Sergeant White. The rock was so big by now that it was almost impossible to carry it and run along with the M14 and backpack. The poor sap with the rock was always last for everything, and nobody said a word or laughed.

Today was payday, so we would have one more chance to beat Snyder in poker, and several of us were waiting.

On our last morning as we waited for Sergeant White, I couldn't stop thinking of Snyder winning at poker once again.

Kenny and I would be going to the same training school because we joined on the Buddy Program. As Sergeant White handed us our orders, he smiled and said, "Good luck." I looked at the orders, which read C. C., Ft. Gordon, Georgia. I thought to myself, how bad could this be? I then asked Sergeant White what it meant. I had no idea how to read orders. The Sergeant smiled again and said, "Camp Crockett."

Camp Crockett was located out of Fort Gordon, Georgia, maybe twenty miles from the base. It was a pre-airborne training school for Vietnam. Both Kenny and I had heard stories about Camp Crockett during the past eight weeks but never really believed that we would be sent there. It's called "Hell on Earth." What were we in for?

I felt my heart sink, and I felt very weak. Nobody else had orders to Camp Crockett, not even the guys that got drafted. How could this happen? Kenny said, "Don't worry about it. At least we'll go together." I thought to myself, *Yes, you could say that, because if it weren't for you, I wouldn't be here in the first place.* But at least we did get thirty days off.

Sergeant White said, "We will not be running this morning. I have done my best to turn you into men in eight weeks, and it turns out that not all of you are men."

Of our original group of twenty-two, we lost three guys to yellow jaundice and one recycle, Raymond, would be spending another eight weeks with Sergeant White and then discharged if he couldn't make it a second time.

The training we had been through was really tough. The adrenalin in my body was rushing, knowing that we get to go home. I had never before felt so strong. Sergeant White said that our group almost looked like soldiers, and if he could have us for another "eight years," he could make men out of all of us.

"One last thing before you go," Sergeant White said, "if any of you did not like your training, or think you are now so tough you can fight me, this is your last chance." One of the guys that said he was going to kick his ass earlier, Big Tom from Texas, stepped forward. Sergeant White looked at him and said, "Are you sure that you want to go home in pieces?" The guy stepped back in formation. "Okay, I'll give you all one more chance together. All of you may attack at once and probably win." Still, nobody moved. This was a good offer, but I certainly wouldn't want to be in the front. Finally, he said, "I must go. I have another bunch of recruits waiting. Goodbye, men, and good luck." Then he walked off.

As Kenny and I sat on the bus waiting for it to take us to the airport, we could see Sergeant White greeting the new bunch of recruits. They were all in civilian clothes, and most had long hair, except for Raymond standing in the middle. Sergeant White was yelling at them as loud as he could. "I have never seen such a poor bunch of recruits. You all look like girls, and it's my job to make men out of you," and then our bus drove off.

CHAPTER 13

ON OUR WAY home, Kenny and I talked about what we would do on leave. We were very excited about seeing our families and friends. We would probably go to Reno with Richard. Maybe I would try to change our ID cards to make us twenty-one years old. I really believed if we were old enough to die for our country, we should be old enough to choose if we want to drink a cold beer.

Mom and Dad were very excited about having me home and hearing all about the stories of basic training. They were planning on a family dinner. Grandma Emily, Dad's mother, and Aunt Lorean, Dad's sister, lived in trailers on the property. They had cold beer waiting and wanted to hear it all. Kenny and I stopped by almost daily for a cold beer and visit. Richard would also join us when he could.

It didn't take long for me to change the ID cards. I peeled off the old lamination with steam from a teapot. They looked fair even though the new lamination that I used from the photo booth at the Greyhound Bus Depot in Marysville was too thick, but they would have to do.

Our family dinner was nice with everyone there, including all three of my sisters and families. Mom had cooked pheasant and dumplings in the pressure cooker with all of the trimmings. After dinner, I called Kenny, and we started planning our next trip to Reno with Richard.

Richard was a senior now, and by the time he graduated, Kenny and I would probably be in Vietnam.

Richard had been working at Del Pero as a meat cutter but quit so that he could go into farming. His grandfather had many acres of nuts and rice. His dad had around 100 acres of prunes. Richard always had a great interest in farming and worked in all phases of it. His dream was to be a "farmer" all of his life.

Driving up to Reno was fun. Snow had been falling on the summit, but not enough to need snow chains. We didn't have much money, but if we didn't win, we could always sleep in the car . . . It wouldn't be the first time.

Arriving in Reno, we had about eighty dollars between us. We all bought a roll of nickels and started playing in front of the waitress so that we could get free drinks. Some of the casinos asked us for identification, and some didn't. Our military ID cards worked fine, but we had to leave anyway because Richard didn't have an ID. It didn't take long until we were about broke. Kenny and I had nothing, and Richard had twenty dollars. We were all pretty buzzed by now because we had been drinking and playing slots for hours.

Richard said, "Look, I'll give you my last twenty dollars, and that way, both you and Kenny would have ten dollars each to make a stand on the Black Jack table, and I'll go sleep in the car. If you win, let me know, and we'll go and check into a hotel."

Kenny and I each took our ten dollars and sat down at a Black Jack (Twenty-One) game in the Nevada Club. Security came right over and asked us for our IDs. He looked very close and then gave them back.

We started playing and winning. We were betting more as they served us more drinks. We were now playing ten- to twenty-dollar hands and winning. Finally, we realized we had a lot of money in front of us. They were changing dealers every five minutes, and we were starting to lose. We cashed out a total of $500. We were on cloud 9. This was too cool. We rushed back to the car where Richard was sleeping and started yelling and screaming that we won! We pressed $500 against the window so that when he awoke, the first thing he saw was money. How exciting. We then split up our winnings and checked into The Travelodge on Fourth Street.

The hotels on Fourth Street were a little run-down but cheap. They charged us an extra five dollars for a roll away bed. We gladly paid so that we all had our own bed. Now, the coin toss, the only fair way to see who sleeps on the roll away. Yes, I was the first one out. Now, it was between Kenny and Richard. As the toss started, Kenny said, "Richard, I'll take the roll away because it can't be as bad as an army bunk," and laughed. Richard liked that idea.

It was great going home winners for a change. With all of us bragging about the money we won in Reno, of course, we were planning another trip.

Our river parties were the same except that most of the girls that I had been dating already had new boyfriends. Joy had a new boyfriend; Cheryl had a new boyfriend who wanted to kick my ass. I told her to get lost and tell her punk boyfriend the same. Peggy had several new boyfriends, and Gerri had just written me a letter before I got out of basic saying that she was moving to Oklahoma to live with her father.

Our friends, Sharon and Virginia, from Live Oak, were still single and wanted to go to the river with us and hear all of our stories from the army.

Another fun night on the river. Richard showed up with a new girlfriend. We had hot dogs and chips around the campfire, along with cold beer—so much fun.

We all shared stories around the campfire. Both Kenny and I told a few stories about basic training and Sergeant White. Richard talked about his farming and planting a new prune orchard.

Time was going by fast, and we had less than one week to report to Camp Crockett. Kenny and I drove up to Reno for the day. If we won again, we were planning on staying over. If not, we would drive back that night. Richard had to work so he couldn't go with us. We started playing Twenty-One at the Nevada Club again, thinking we might win there, but we didn't. Our luck was as bad as it could get, and it wasn't long until we were almost broke.

Kenny suggested taking in some of the nightclubs with the last of our money instead of giving it to the casinos. Our ID cards had been working great. We took in several nightclubs, and some of them had topless dancers like the ones we saw in Oakland.

We walked into a club, and the bartender asked us for our ID cards. He took the cards over to a table with a strong light. Then he walked back over to us and said, "These cards look good, but I spent over twenty years in the Marines, and I know these have been re-laminated. Now, I'll give you a choice: turn around and walk out of here without your cards, or I'll call the military police and let them decide."

We turned around and ran out without our ID cards. This was terrible. Now we wouldn't have our cards when we checked into Camp Crockett. We had no choice. We had to tell a small lie. When we checked into Camp Crockett, we'd need to say that we were held up at gunpoint, and we both lost our wallets.

Cheryl called and said her boyfriend Billy wanted to fight me. He blamed me for breaking them up last year. He had been boxing all of his senior year, thinking of me. Billy was on the telephone, cussing at me and calling me names. He was at her house and waiting for me to arrive.

Kenny rode with me to Cheryl's house. He said that he had my back if more than one attacked me. Billy was waiting at Cheryl's door. He outweighed me by at least forty pounds. Two other guys were in the living room. As we approached the door, Billy said, "To the backyard, shit face." I never said a word. We all walked through the house and out into the backyard.

As soon as I stepped off the porch, he attacked. His blows were fierce, and he fought like a boxer. I was completely on the defence, blocking his blows until I quickly realized I couldn't just stand and box with him. I kicked him as hard as I could, again and again. I was using sidekicks to the knee, and then I knew I had him as he almost dropped with a kick between the legs. All of a sudden, we heard police cars screaming in front of the house. I kicked Billy again and again, and Kenny yelled, "Stop, it's the police!" Billy was bleeding from the nose and mouth. His friends ran out the back gate, and Billy limped out.

My car was parked in front, so we had no choice but to go out the front. As it turned out, the police were going to the neighbor's house, because the old lady next door had a heart attack.

We ended the fight with all of us sneaking off. On the ride home, Kenny said, "You actually scared me when you started kicking that guy with your combat boots. You looked just like Sergeant White! That guy is going to be hurting later." We both laughed. I then realized why Sergeant White pushed us so hard.

Later, Cheryl called and said that Billy claimed that I had cheated by kicking him and that he could have beaten me in a fair fight. I told her that she deserved Billy and never to call me again. I also told her to tell Billy that there's no such thing as a fair fight. She did say that the lady next door who had the heart attack had it just before we arrived, so it wasn't us who caused it. I was glad to know that.

Our time was running out, but we had a wedding to attend. My sister, Arvella, married Robert Armstrong. The wedding was held at my sister, Nadine's house in the backyard—a beautiful and festive day. Kenny and I wore our uniforms. Most of the family and lots of friends were there. It was a wonderful day to remember.

CHAPTER 14

Suddenly, our thirty-day leave was over. We were now on our way to Camp Crockett. We flew to Atlanta, Georgia, and took a bus to Fort Gordon. When we checked in at the gate, the guard looked at our orders and laughed. "You're going to Camp Crockett." He pointed at a truck and said to get in the back with the other poor slobs going to Crockett. As we drove out the gates, the driver yelled to us, "Be sure to take a good look at Fort Gordon because you won't see it again for eight more weeks, as you are all "Going to Hell."

Luckily, the guard at the gate never did ask us for our IDs after looking at our orders for Camp Crockett.

The road was beginning to get very rough. I wondered if the driver was trying to throw us out. It was freezing in the back of the truck, and I kept thinking how nice it would be to get to Crockett and warm up. I mean, really, how bad could it be? We had already lived through basic with Sergeant White.

All of a sudden, these round metal Quonset huts appeared and an old sign that read, "*CAMP CROCKETT.*"

The truck stopped. A man yelled, "Get your ass off my truck now. Move, move." Then another man about six foot two with several scars on his face walked up. It was our new drill instructor, Sergeant Knoll, telling us what we were in for. He was speaking loudly but not screaming at us.

"Men, you are here to learn how to kill, and some of you *will* be killed. It's my job to teach you how to stay alive. This is Sergeant Townsend, and both of us are into the martial arts. We both enjoy karate. Anytime you don't like something, just speak up, and we'll kick your ass, and this may become 'daily' for some of you."

The second DI, Sergeant Townsend, pushed one of the guys to the ground and said, "Don't ever grin when one of us is talking to you. Now, get up, fuck head." He stood as ordered, and the DI pushed him again. DI Townsend was a little shorter, about six feet even, and a real snake.

The rest of us were standing there like we were frozen, and it was so cold, I thought we were going to freeze in place. Finally, the first DI said, "Follow me, and I'll show you to your quarters." The metal Quonset hut was freezing. After the DI walked off, we all rushed over to light the stove. As the heat came out, so did a layer of black soot. It reminded me of smudging pots used by the farmers to keep their crops from freezing in the wintertime.

Welcome to Camp Crockett, a dirty, stinking, run-down, and disgusting place to be.

Just before daylight, Sergeant Knoll came into the hut, yelling, "Get your ass out of bed now. Move, move!" When I jumped from the bunk, I noticed a layer of black soot covering everything, including my face. Both Kenny and I ran to the showers. Cold water only, and near freezing. It took my breath away when I first got in. Kenny was really cussing about it. Worse yet, the seats at the outhouses were also freezing.

As we all stood at attention, the first DI asked, "What do you all want to do today?" None of us said a word, but I was thinking, *Spend the day indoors.*

Then he yelled, "Kill, kill, kill. Now, what do you want to do today?"

We all yelled, "Kill, kill, kill."

He yelled again, louder, "Kill, kill, kill. Now, whenever I ask you, 'What you want to do today?' or we pass another unit, you had better yell louder than they do. What will I hear?"

We all yelled, "Kill, kill, kill!"

He said both he and Sergeant Townsend had served in Vietnam, and they both loved to kill. They seemed so full of hate. They also had several other trainers with them that all looked like they just got out of prison.

Sergeant Knoll wanted to fight someone really badly. He was getting louder as he explained what hell he was going to put us through. He would work us from daylight to dark in the beginning and sometimes fourteen hours a day. There would be no day off for the married men, and no one except the deathly ill or dead could leave Camp Crockett at all. If anybody tried to go AWOL and were caught, they would be shot, and if they lived, they would wish they had died. This was not like basic training where, if you failed, they would recycle you to go through the training again. You would either make it here—or you would die.

Again, he yelled, "Now, what do you want to do today?"

We all yelled, "Kill, kill, kill!"

"Louder!"

"Kill, kill, kill!!!"

"Now, we're going to do twenty push-ups, run five miles, and then we get a three-minute breakfast." I could see right now that Camp Crockett was going to be terrible.

Well, I was right. We had now been here a week, and this was pure hell. We were averaging about four hours of sleep a night. We were in live fire, hand-to-hand combat, exercises, survival classes, war games, and cussed at, all day long. It was so cold, freezing, actually, with ice on the ground. This was February at Camp Crockett, Georgia.

Rumor had it that we were the last class to go through Camp Crockett, as several deaths were being investigated, including some drill instructors. Someone disappeared every week or so, and nobody ever heard from them again. It seemed that DIs would take problem students out for "individual training," and they did not return. The whole place lived in constant fear.

We had finally lost a man out of our barracks. The DIs took him away.

It started at the chow hall. Sergeant Knoll began pushing this Mexican guy, Carlos, who spoke very little English. Sergeant Knoll pushed him again and again, like he was starting a fight, and all of a sudden, Carlos began to punch Sergeant Knoll like he was a punching bag. His blows were so fast and powerful that Sergeant Knoll could not defend himself, and he went down. At the same time, Carlos fell to the ground with a very hard kick in the back from Sergeant Townsend. All four of the trainers started kicking him. Carlos could no longer fight. Sergeant Townsend smashed his head into the ground so hard we all thought he was dead. The guy just lay there, unconscious, with blood all over. Sergeant Knoll, now back on his feet, yelled at us all to return to our barracks until further notice. "Now, move, move."

We all ran to our barracks.

We were all talking about the fight. One man who could speak Spanish said that Carlos was a heavyweight champion fighter from Puerto Rico. No wonder he could fight so well.

Hours passed. This was the longest break we had had at Camp Crockett. Some guys were playing cards, some writing letters, and some were catching a wink while they could. Evening finally came, and Sergeant Knoll came in, yelling to fall out for dinner. He looked as if he had been beaten with a baseball bat. One eye was almost swollen shut. He said that Sergeant Townsend had taken Carlos into Fort Gordon to the hospital. He promised if the guy came back, we would all get to see the rematch. He said, "I will stomp him into the ground."

Nights were getting worse.

We had learned the hard way not to go outside at night, not even to the outhouse. We could hear the moans and beatings of the ones that were caught venturing out. One guy who was severely beaten claimed he was also "raped." Kenny and I were terrified. We needed to stay together and fight.

"Kill, kill, kill."

The cold was unbearable.

Morning came early with very little sleep. I was coughing from all of the soot from the night before. The hatred was building rapidly. Other units were also becoming our enemies.

As we passed them, we yelled, "Kill, kill kill!"

They did the same.

"Kill, kill, kill." Each unit competed to be the loudest. War games with the other units were becoming all-out fights, and we were always expected to win. Hand-to-hand combat was no longer practiced. It was real, with guys being carried off by the medics on stretchers all day. It was true . . . Guys were not coming back, including Carlos, who beat up Sergeant Knoll. One day, all of his gear just disappeared, and he never returned.

Several guys had tried to go AWOL and were caught. All were beaten severely, and one was supposedly taken to the hospital but never returned. Kenny and I were also trying to think of a way to escape. These people were inhumane. This could not be standard military training. The hatred was now so bad that everyone wanted to kill somebody. *"Kill, kill, kill"* is all we thought about all day. Of course, all of the married guys had been convinced that "Jody" was having sex with their wives while they were away. The only thing to do was kill Jody on the way to Vietnam. They were told continuously that Jody was sleeping with their wives. And what do you want to do to Jody? *"Kill, kill kill."*

It looked like Kenny and I were going to get our chance to escape. Sergeant Knoll told us that we would both be on KP duty (kitchen patrol) for one day. At 2:00 p.m., there would be a truck going to Fort Gordon, and he wanted us to ride into the fort and get new military

ID cards. I had told him on our first day that we both had lost our ID cards when we were robbed at gunpoint in Reno. Sergeant Knoll said that we shouldn't have given up our wallets. We should have attacked the robber, and for not doing that, we both had to drop down and give him twenty push-ups.

The truck wouldn't be returning to Crockett, so we were expected to find our own way back and should be back no later than 8:00 p.m.

KP duty is like a day off. Even though the cook works you all day without a break, peeling potatoes, washing pots and pans, etc., it was still a holiday compared to being out in the field with those maniacs. At 2:00 p.m., we told the cook we had to leave to catch the truck into Fort Gordon.

This was great. We would get our new ID cards and then walk right off the base. We were thinking maybe of going to Canada. We knew we could not go home being AWOL because the military police would be looking for us. Kenny had already warned his parents in a letter that things were so bad here that we might leave. He claimed that even his dad would understand when he explained how inhumanely we were treated.

It didn't take long to get issued new ID cards, and Kenny was dying for a cold brew. Well, we got away with it in basic, so we decided to go to the Enlisted Men's Club for a cold one.

I asked where the EM Club was located. It was only about a mile away. It didn't take us long to make our way over to the club, and we proceeded to down a few cold ones. We were trying to decide what to do. Our training at Camp Crockett was almost half over, but we might not get another chance to escape. We really believed guys were dying there, and we don't want to be one of them.

Well, after a few cold ones, we were feeling a little tougher, like maybe we could go back to Camp Crockett and survive. The cocktail waitress asked us if we would like another round. I thought I would make a joke and pulled my finger off in front of her (a trick I learned as a little boy) and told her it was shot off in Vietnam. She screamed and dropped her tray. Drinks splashed everywhere, and the bouncers (military police) were there instantly.

The MPs took Kenny and I outside of the EM Club. I explained what had happened. It was only a joke, and I pulled my finger off for them. They asked what unit we were with. When I told them we were training at Camp Crockett, they wanted to know how we got away from there. They were shocked that anyone got away from Crockett. I explained the ID card situation to them, and they realized we had already missed our curfew. They felt sorry for us. One of the MPs offered to give us a ride in the patrol car back to Camp Crockett.

He was an older guy, maybe forty-five years old with a thick, black mustache. He took us within a mile and told us we would have to walk from here, as he could not be seen driving to Camp Crockett in the patrol car. As we got out of the car, he said, "I feel sorry for you, boys. I have heard some of the horror stories coming out of Crockett. Good luck to both of you." What a nice guy. The first one that I had ever met in the military.

It was 2320 hours (11:20 p.m.) when we finally walked into Camp Crockett. As we neared the guardhouse, we could see the lights on, and a couple of guys sitting at a table. We crept by, hoping not to be noticed. Of course, all of the lights in our barracks were out, so we had to be very quiet so that no one would know what time we arrived.

Morning came early, as usual, and no one was aware of how late we had come in last night. Both Kenny and I felt like we had been on vacation. Just one night away made us realize how lucky we had been and decided that we could make it through this. I mean, nobody gets a night out drinking when they're at Camp Crockett.

We realized that this would never happen again. Camp Crockett is miles away from Fort Gordon. It would be almost impossible to sneak out of Camp Crockett at night and go into Fort Gordon.

There were now two guys missing from our barracks. One of the guys told us that Sergeant Knoll came in last night and removed their belongings. No one knew where they went, and no one asked. Maybe it was time that someone should ask. But perhaps we didn't want to know.

Every day . . . *kill, kill, kill.*

The units were all fighting one another.

One morning as I tried to leave the outhouse, the door would not open. When I pushed it harder, I could see some guys holding it on the other side. I screamed, "Let me out of here," and kicked the door as hard as I could. The door went flying open, and I was facing four guys from another unit. I kicked the first one in front of me, only to be hit and kicked from both sides. I hit and kicked again before I went down. As soon as I hit the ground, I heard Kenny yelling, "Ike, are you OK?"

I looked up to see Kenny standing over me with about ten of our guys. The other unit ran when they saw Kenny coming with so many. Kenny helped me up, but I was really hurt. I told him that I might have broken ribs from being kicked. He said that I was actually on the ground a couple of minutes before he got to me. I thought it was only a matter of seconds, but it was just as well that I didn't remember, as I was also bleeding from the mouth and nose.

Kenny helped me to my bunk. Not long after, Sergeant Knoll came in and asked me how I was feeling. When I told him, he said that I needed to get up and give him twenty push-ups for losing the fight. I told him I couldn't do it. He looked at me, paused for a moment, and said, "OK, but you owe me twenty-five," and walked out. Kenny thought that I should have demanded to go to the hospital.

The next day, I did get to see the medic. He said that I did not have any broken bones, only bruises with a swollen face. Upon hearing this, Sergeant Knoll said, "You better keep up with the unit, or you **will** have broken bones." Kenny said that he was prepared to fight Sergeant Knoll if he hit me or kicked me.

It was difficult keeping up with my unit as sore as I was. "Kill, kill, kill" is all we heard all day long. It was all we were allowed to think about. *Kill, kill, kill.*

That day was live fire again, but this time, only four inches above us. As I lay on the ground with bullets flying over me, all I could think of was how much I hated Sergeant Knoll.

This was the worst place I had ever been in my life. This made basic training seem like a vacation. It was freezing cold all the time. No hot water, it smelled of sewage, fights occurred every day, and inhumane training to boot. The food was sickening, and I could usually eat almost anything. The mess shack was truly a shack and very unclean. The fear and hatred was building up in all of us.

Our normal day was now about fourteen hours of pure misery. Our hand-to-hand training now included "deathblows to the nose" and breaking of the neck. We practiced these blows on dummies. I was surprised that Sergeant Knoll didn't have us practice on each other. We now fought each other until one dropped to the ground. I understood now why we were the last unit to go through Camp Crockett. Nobody should be treated like this.

Kill, kill, kill.

We lost another man last night. Big Mouth Ted, who was always right no matter what you were talking about. He had been getting into daily yelling matches with both drill instructors and was chosen for "special" guard duty a couple of nights ago. Nobody had seen him since. Last night, his personal items were removed, and we were told he had "the fever." We had been informed in the beginning, if you got "the fever," you would disappear.

With only two more weeks at Camp Crockett, it was time to make a decision. We could apply for another school, but the only one being offered was Chemical Warfare. Jump school was not being offered, as Airborne units in Vietnam were not jumping at all due to the jungles. In Vietnam, Airborne units were working like Air Mobile units. We were told, "If we lived through Vietnam, we could jump and get our wings after we returned to the States." Sergeant Knoll promised in the beginning that any of us who survived his training would either go to another school or take a thirty-day leave and then on to Vietnam. I didn't like the sound of another school. I had thought basic training was bad . . . until I arrived at Camp Crockett!

Yes, I would go to Vietnam. It couldn't be any worse than Camp Crockett.

Kenny chose chemical training, and he would get a thirty-day leave after Camp Crockett. He thought I should have chosen it also, saying, "How bad could it be?" It would keep him out of Vietnam another three months. I told him, "I will not take that chance." What if it turned out to be another Camp Crockett? I would much rather be in Vietnam. This school had truly achieved what it wanted. The hatred was sky high, and we still ran around all day, yelling, "Kill, kill, kill." Killing is all that mattered. Some of the guys had gone overboard. I heard them say who they were going to kill on the way to Vietnam. I wondered if all of our American troops were trained this way, or was it Camp Crockett. I sure hoped when I got to Vietnam; I didn't end up in a unit with maniacs like some of these guys were turning into.

During our last week, we would all be in survival training. It was so cold outside with snow on the ground. The training was intense, more push-ups, more running, more fighting, and more kill, kill, kill. The hatred was so high that we were now afraid of our own men.

Kenny had KP duty again. He only worked for twelve hours that day, so I thought he had a day off. He did get to know one of the cooks who sold him a pint of whiskey. Jim Beam, one of Kenny's favorites. He said, "We'll drink it tomorrow night when we have our compass reading night."

We had been informed that compass reading would be at night many miles from Camp Crockett. We would have all night to get back to camp using the compass, but we mustn't get caught.

A team of instructors would be hunting us down like animals, and if we were caught, we would get "torture training." The ones who got caught or surrendered would be put in cages . . . "Viet Cong" style.

I couldn't believe that we had to go through this and in the snow. Sleep did not come easy, as I was so worried about the next night.

Morning came with the usual screaming and yelling, "Kill, kill,

kill." It was working. The guys were serious when yelling, "Kill."

That night arrived quickly, and most of us were already exhausted from the day. We had spent all day on the firing range, shooting at various targets as we yelled, "kill, kill, kill." Kenny seemed to have lots of energy. Knowing he would have a taste of whiskey was giving him a great push.

We were all loaded up in the back of trucks like cattle. We all had a compass and knew how to read it from the compass class a few days ago. The trucks drove for about forty-five minutes before coming to a stop. We were all told to get out. "Now move, move, you bunch of sissies!"

Sgt. Knoll said: "You do have all night to get back to camp, but you may want to get back quickly because of the cold." He informed us that if anyone tried to follow the road back and got caught, they would be "tortured." "Stay in the woods and follow your compass."

As everyone started out, Kenny and I dropped back. We hid in the trees and watched for Sgt. Knoll to come out and start chasing. He never got out of the truck.

Kenny and I were both enjoying the warm whiskey on such a cold night. Finally, the truck started up and drove away. We'd finished about half of the pint when we both decided to sneak back to camp following the road. When we saw headlights, we'd both get off the road into the brush. It was really freezing. I couldn't imagine doing this without a pint of whiskey.

After several hours of walking, knowing we were within a couple of miles of Camp Crockett, we went back into the snow-covered woods. Our whiskey bottle was now gone, but Kenny said this was the best he had felt in months. I actually felt warm myself, but we had walked for miles. At least, this was a clear night so we could see where we were walking.

We arrived back at camp around 0100 hours (1:00 a.m.). The camp was totally quiet. I thought we would get caught returning to our huts, but nobody was awake. We snuck in and went to our bunks.

We did hear other guys coming in during the night and complaining how hard it was walking back through the snow-covered woods. We made it and never got caught.

The next day, we received our orders. Most all of us were Vietnam bound except for a few like Kenny, who chose chemical school. We would both get a thirty-day leave, so we'd be able to go home together. Kenny would report to chemical warfare training after our leave. I would have chosen jump school if it were still being offered. At this point, I would rather face Vietnam than another school, especially chemicals.

We were thinking of taking the bus from Atlanta, Georgia, to New Orleans, and then flying home from there. That should be a lot of fun, and it was sure nice to think of fun again with Camp Crockett almost over.

Later that day, I received my shots for Vietnam. Both arms ached from so many shots. Basic training shots were nothing compared to this. Both of my arms were dripping with blood. I thought I was going to throw up but didn't.

We had little time to pack our bags before Sgt. Knoll called us to attention. We were all standing there frozen from the cold. Sgt. Knoll said, "Today, I release you to your own future. Most of you are going straight to Vietnam. Many of you will die. I hope that some of you will live because of my training."

Sgt. Townsend then stepped up, and Sgt. Knoll walked off. Sgt. Townsend told us there was a bus waiting at the front gate. The bus would take us all to Fort Gordon and turn us "free" for our thirty-day leave.

There was no goodbye. He just walked off. True to their nature, neither drill instructor wavered. They were both jerks to the end.

On the bus, some guys talked about going back to Camp Crockett and stomping both sergeants into the ground. They wanted us all to be able to kill and to hate, and we do hate—we all hate them!!

Several of us decided to stop at the EM Club for a few beers. Kenny was dying for a cold one. We drank a few beers and waited for our bus. We had decided to ride the bus as far as New Orleans.

Chapter 15

THE BUS STOPPED every hour somewhere, but we did manage to catch some sleep. At this point, we could sleep almost anywhere, as we were both so exhausted from Camp Crockett.

The Southern states were a real experience to ride a bus through. I was surprised and shocked to see that the drinking establishments had signs on the front doors reading, "*White Only*" or "*Black Only*." I had never seen this before.

We were sure glad to get to New Orleans, where we checked into a cheap hotel on Bourbon Street. New Orleans was really happening, with music on the streets, dancing, and bars as far as you could see. We decided to have a drink at different bars and make our way up Bourbon Street until we ran out of money. The night was lively, with most places having music, dancers, strippers, and a very rowdy crowd.

When morning came, I found Kenny sitting on the bathroom floor close to the toilet, vomiting as he had been throughout the night. I wasn't much better. I guess we had too much fun.

Later, after we recovered, we decided to go our separate ways. Kenny would fly home. I would take the bus to Oklahoma to see a girlfriend, Gerri, who had just moved there from California to be with her father.

Gerri and her cousin picked me up at the bus station in Hugo, Oklahoma. Gerri was happy to see me, and her family were all very nice. After arriving at their home, I asked to use the restroom. Gerri got up and walked out of the room. Her father said, "She's a little embarrassed," as they only had an outhouse in the backyard.

I told him that was fine, as I had just spent eight weeks using an outhouse, so I was used to it.

We laughed about that later and had a wonderful three days. We drove around a lot and talked. Gerri seemed to want to tell me about her entire life. I got to know her more in those three days than I did when I dated her in California. The only thing that she would not talk about was our first date. When we were kissing at a party, she went limp, like she passed out. I thought she was faking it, but she turned sort of blue. Her girlfriend, Kathy, stepped in and said to let her lie there a few minutes, and she would be all right. Kathy said this happened to her all the time in school.

My short trip to Oklahoma was now over, and Gerri took me to the bus station. As I got on the bus, she started to cry and said that she would write to me in Vietnam. With tears in her eyes, she said, "I hope I'll be here when you come home."

I thought I knew what she meant. I was trained! I knew she meant she would be with "Jody" and not waiting for me when I came home. Oh well, I didn't expect her to wait anyway.

Arriving home was wonderful, as always. Mom and Dad were eagerly waiting for me. The hunting dogs in the front yard were all barking, and Gigi, our miniature poodle, was in the house jumping up and down. My grandmother was calling to me from her trailer to come and see her, and so was my aunt from the other trailer. The excitement was overwhelming. Mom was planning a large venison dinner for the family and friends.

Mom also saved me a couple of copies of a poem that I had written and sent home from Camp Crockett. It was published in our local newspaper, the *Live Oak Acorn*.

A Soldier's Thoughts before Going to Vietnam

As I lay at night awake, always wondering of my fate.
I will always remember the fun I've had.
Never forget hunting with Dad.
All soldiers say they will do their best.
And we all hope to pass that test.
Some men have wives and kids at home.
Yet, they are here to stand alone.
Training was tough, learning to kill
Destiny is now in God's will.
I know I will see tracers, mortars, and bombs.
For this place I am going is called Vietnam.

Now that I had been home for a few days, the reality was starting to set in. When I leave this time—it is for real.

Kenny was also home, and we were planning a trip to Reno. This time, we would wear our uniforms, hoping that we would not get carded for our age. Richard was going with us. I had a spare uniform, so we decided to dress him up in a uniform too. The uniform was new with no rank or ribbons whatsoever on it. That would not do, as both Kenny and I had our Private E2 stripe and shooting badges, but we had no extras. There was no army base near Live Oak, but there was an air base (Beale Air Base) close to us, so I thought, why not drive over to the air base and buy a few ribbons? I mean, really, who would ever pay any attention in Reno?

We drove to Beale Air Base, handed the guard our army IDs, and drove to the PX (Post Exchange).

Well, we did it. We bought a few air force ribbons and badges and put them on Richard's army uniform. We also bought him a nice maroon beret. Not sure what it meant, but Richard sure looked authentic wearing it.

Reno was fun. Richard looked so silly wearing this mix and match uniform, but it was working. Nobody was asking us for IDs. We were having a great time playing slots and ordering drinks. Then, Richard came up to me, almost frantic. He said a man was asking questions, and he did not know what to say. He wanted to know, "What the hell I am?" I looked past Richard, and about ten feet away was a man about forty years old with a shaved head, and he looked like he was made out of steel.

I asked Richard who he was. He said the guy claimed to be a Captain with the Army Special Forces.

I thought, *Oh no, he's a Green Beret*, and I yelled, "Run!"

We ran out of the casino so fast that a few people fell down in our path, making it difficult for him to catch us. We ran across the street to the Primadonna Casino, and, yes, he was coming after us. We ran out the back, down the alley, through a few of the small casinos, and over to the Mapes Casino. Thinking we'd thrown him off, we ordered a beer and watched all the doors, waiting for him to enter. Richard wanted to make a stand and fight him.

I warned him, "Don't even think about it. This guy is one of the army's best fighters."

A short time passed, and he didn't enter, so we ordered another beer. It was a quick one, though, as there he was on the far side of the casino. Luckily, he didn't see us. We ran out the back and up the street through the Club Cal Neva and over to Harrah's Casino. From there, we decided to give up and go to the car. We snuck out the back of Harrah's and over to the parking lot.

We thought about going to Sparks and playing a little more but changed our minds and headed for California. Richard was worried that his uniform would get us caught. Then we all busted out laughing. We did stop at Bill & Effie's for coffee, but Richard stayed in the car.

We got our coffee to go and were on our way.

This was not the kind of night that I had expected in Reno. I was hoping to get a hotel room and spend the night. Oh well, at least, we were all getting home in one piece, and we laughed all the way home. Richard looked so funny in that mismatched uniform.

Time was going by fast, and I only had a few days free now.

Kenny was also getting ready to leave for his next school. When I was alone or in bed, Vietnam entered my thoughts. I was terrified, but I didn't show it, of course, in front of other people.

Kenny and Richard got a few other friends together for a party on the river bottom for me. We all had a few beers. Everyone was talking about me leaving for Vietnam. A few of the girls were crying, but all had a good time . . . Except for me, as I was crying on the inside because *I* was the one out of time. It was real. I was going to Vietnam.

As I drove home late that night, I kept playing the new hit song by the Rolling Stones, "Out of Time," on my new 8-track as tears poured down my face. The song seemed to fit me so well.

Goodbyes were always hard, but this was the worst. Everyone was crying but trying to cheer me up by saying, "You'll make it; you'll be fine." Mom was trying to keep Dad calm, as he had just been diagnosed with a heart problem. Now, I would have that to worry about that as well.

My folks drove me to Travis Air Base to catch my flight. It was true. I was going to Vietnam. We said our goodbyes, and Mom was crying. I knew she was very worried about me. Dad just shook my hand, and when we made eye contact, I could see the tears. All of the guys there were going to Nam. What a sober bunch of faces standing in line to get on the plane.

It was a military transport plane, and we sat on the floor strapped to the walls. Very uncomfortable. We also had no windows to look out of. We just stared at each other. The plane flew over Alaska and Japan. It took two days to reach Nam. The engine was so loud I could hardly hear myself think.

Reaching Alaska was nice as we were allowed off the plane for an hour. Some of the guys called home one last time, but most of us just sat around and talked about what was in front of us and where we were going. Most of us would be assigned to units upon arrival in the country. We never got off the plane in Japan; only refuelled . . . and then on to Vietnam.

CHAPTER 16

WE LANDED AT Tan Son Nhut Air Base, in southern Vietnam near Saigon, under mortar fire. The base had been hit all night with mortars. You could hear rifle fire in the distance and explosions all around. We were instructed to depart the plane onto large trucks to take us to Long Binh Army Base. We were told it was about an hour's drive from Saigon. The two-and-a-half ton trucks looked like cattle trucks but were filled with soldiers. As we drove out of the air base, we entered Saigon.

What a mess. Thousands of people in the streets, walking, riding bicycles, motorized bicycles with a seat on the back for passengers, and cars. It seemed nobody paid any attention to stop signs. You go when you can. It was hot, and the smell was overwhelming. It smelled like spoiled food. It stank. The poverty here was something one must see to believe: shacks everywhere, and women squatting down on the street to urinate. The poor have no running water.

We crossed a bridge, and the river was lined with people washing clothes and living on the riverbanks. The water looked very polluted and had a foul smell. I'd always heard that Saigon was a beautiful city, but not now. I was sure glad to get out of Saigon and on our way to Long Binh.

I worried all the way that we would be shot before reaching Long Binh. American helicopters were flying around everywhere, so I thought maybe if we get shot at, the helicopters would come to our rescue. We passed many rice fields, and we could see a lonely farmer working his rice by hand.

It was a relief to see Long Binh in the distance. There seemed to be a lot of black smoke going up into the sky, but I thought that might be normal. As we went through the gates, I remembered my mother telling me about her cousin getting killed in Korea. He died his first week.

Well, I made it to Long Binh. This camp stinks worse than Saigon, but I was soon to find the reason for that.

It was getting dark and starting to rain; yet, it seemed so warm. At least, I was not freezing my butt off like at Camp Crockett. We were told to unload and line up for processing. We heard an explosion, and the sirens started to howl. The Viet Cong were hitting the base with mortars. It must be our welcoming party. We all hit the ground and were told to keep moving to the chow hall, as there weren't enough bunkers to hold all of us anyway.

Once inside, food was given to us . . . a potato with gravy and corn, and cots with one blanket each. I could hear some guys complaining about the gravy that was tasteless, but I was happy to have it. We were told we would process in the morning and not to worry about the mortars, as we would get used to it.

None of us could sleep as we lay there all night listening to the whistle of the mortars coming in and then exploding. I wondered why they wouldn't build more bunkers. How could they make us lie in these bunks with no protection?

We could hear gunfire in the distance, which we later found out, was the US Army firing on the Viet Cong, or "Charlie," as they were also known by. All of a sudden, there was a loud explosion, and the roof started pounding. We all thought we had been hit!

I fell off my cot. There was a lot of screaming.

But it was only rain. I had never heard rain like that before. What a downpour. It was raining so hard you couldn't hear the sirens or the mortars. Once I realized it was just the rain, I fell asleep for a few hours. I always did sleep well in the rain.

Up early and very happy to be alive, I started the morning with a fast breakfast of scrambled powdered eggs and toast, but I wasn't complaining, as it did fill the void. Today, I thought we would be getting our orders and clothes issued and be moving on to our units. We were told that it could be days or a week before we arrived at our units.

I wondered about Kenny. He must be in chemical warfare school by now.

Our time at Long Binh Army Base would be spent working on the base. I thought that this might be good for a few days and might even be fun.

Wrong!

Our sergeant in command walked us to the far backside of the base to show us where we would be working. This was where all of the black smoke was coming from that I could see as we drove onto the base and the stench that had hit me.

There were rows of fifty-five-gallon drums with black smoke pouring out of them, and the smell was enough to make you lose your stomach. It was human waste. Yes, shit mixed with oil and on fire. It would be our job to burn it down and stir it all day long—unbelievable!

We were all assigned to two rows of barrels, ten in each row. There were no septic tanks on the base, and this was the only way to get rid of it. All new enlisted men coming through the base would do this until they were assigned to a unit. After stirring poop for a few hours, we were all black with soot, and imagine what this soot was made of. The only white part on me was my eyeballs. Gross!

When they gave us a lunch break, it was very difficult to eat. Most of us just sat there, staring down at our food. The afternoon was just as bad, adding more oil, adding more waste, and stirring. We were all hoping to get our orders to leave tomorrow—but nobody did. We all did this for three days, and it never got any better.

Finally, after the third day, we were told in the morning to fall out in formation. Some of us would be getting our orders to leave. The sergeant in command called "Attention!" A major then walked up to us and said that before he reads off the names and assignments, that he would explain how it worked.

"First, I will read off five names leaving to the 101st Airborne. These men will be transferred over to Bien Hoa Army Base for orientation and then flown up to their units. They will fill positions that are the most dangerous, working in small teams doing recon patrols (search-and-destroy missions) up by the DMZ (Demilitarized Zone). The rest of you will be assigned later in the week to other areas of work needed, such as the motor pool or other on-base jobs."

I thought to myself, *Yes, with all of the GIs here, I should have a good chance of getting a base job, please, please!*

Oh no, the first name called out to the 101st Airborne was mine! No! No! How could this happen? There must be over a hundred other GIs here, and it's me, the first name called. I could almost cry. Thoughts were rushing through my mind of home, the field, and then home again. None of the other guys looked very thrilled either after getting their assignments.

We were all transported to Bien Hoa Army Base for processing. As we rode over in the back of a truck, no one spoke a word—only blank faces. We just sat there, thinking of our lives and what may be in front of us.

The ride to Bien Hoa Army Base was actually short. Within an hour, we were there. As we entered the base, we were instructed where to go to check in for processing.

The base was made up of Quonset huts and barbed wire. We were told the base gets hit almost daily with mortar fire. We were assigned to a bunk in a hut and told to meet at 0700 hours the following morning for orientation to the 101st Airborne. This gave me a little time to explore this base. I quickly found the EM Club and stopped in for a cold brew. Even though it was only three in the afternoon, the club was hopping. Most of the guys were either en route to or from their units. This was like a transfer base to the 101st Airborne and other units.

Then the sirens started. "Incoming" was announced over a loudspeaker.

All of us in the EM Club were instructed to fall out into the nearest bunker. *Boom. Boom. Boom.* Mortars fell inside the base.

Between the blasts of mortar fire, we all got into a bunker. I was scared until one of the guys said, "Relax. It won't last long now because we can hear the US gunships in the air."

Sure enough, it ended as fast as it had started, and over the loudspeaker, we heard, as the sirens stopped, "You may now resume your duties."

It was getting close to chow time, so I walked over to the mess hall just as it was opening. I asked what was for dinner and was told fried liver. Oh well, it's a good thing that I can eat almost anything.

Actually, it was not that bad. At least it was a hot meal. When you leave the mess hall with your tray empty, some old Vietnamese ladies were by the garbage cans collecting all of the unwanted food. It was a shame that so many guys stuck cigarette butts in their leftover food before dumping them into the cans—sort of gross and sad. The poor Vietnamese will make meals with whatever was left.

After dinner, I headed back to the EM Club. A Vietnamese band was playing popular American songs, and it was great. When the band was on break, I tried talking with one of the girl singers and quickly found out that they only imitate American songs. They cannot speak English.

After leaving the EM Club, I stopped at the PX and bought a small book on Vietnamese. I wanted to start learning the language. I planned to study it daily.

Sirens again? Incoming mortars!

All of us headed once again to the bunkers. *Boom, boom, boom* . . . again and again.

I could hear the gunships in the air and firing out in front of the perimeter. This one lasted longer. It seemed like forever, but it was only about an hour. When the sirens finally ended, I headed for my bunk. I was sleeping in my clothes in case I had to get up quickly and head for a bunker. Once more, the sirens started in the middle of the night. I grabbed my boots and ran to my assigned bunker. Once again, it seemed to last forever.

The night was totally lit up by choppers, flares and mortars. None of the mortars landed close to us. We were so lucky. Finally, the sirens stopped, and the night became quiet.

I went back into my hooch (sleeping area), knowing this might be a long night.

The hooch was a rounded metal building (Quonset hut) with about twenty of us sleeping there. We sectioned off our own space with a blanket, about a five- x ten-foot space. We all had some type of radio. I only had a transistor. Most of us were white, but we did have two Black guys and several Mexicans. All of the Mexicans were from California; both Black guys were from the South, not far from New Orleans. Sgt. White was right about color or race, in Vietnam you must all stick together like brothers!

Sure enough, I was in the bunker several more times. When daylight finally appeared, I felt as if I had been up all night. After a quick shower and breakfast at the mess hall, I lined up with the others for our orientations . . . 0700 and all were present.

We were quickly escorted to a Quonset hut with metal fold-up chairs as our classroom. We sat and listened to a Sergeant telling us what it might be like living out in the field, and that's where we were going. There were about ten of us in the class, all going to different units. We would be getting our orders later that night or the next morning and then departing. After about two hours of classroom discussion, we got a ten-minute break—a quick break and then back into the Quonset hut classroom.

As soon as all of us were back into our chairs, the door flew open. A VC (Viet Cong) armed with an AK-47 ran through the door and yelled, "Get on floor or die! Get on floor or die! Now!"

We all dove for the floor, and then he fired rounds over our heads. We all knew this could be the end. All of a sudden, the instructor walked in and told us this was part of our training.

"Always remember that you can be hit anytime or anywhere, so always be prepared."

I thought to myself, *How could you be prepared for something like this?* We had no weapons and were sitting in a classroom.

I did not daydream the rest of the day. Instead, I felt about half sick with worry.

That night was about the same as the night before . . . back to the EM Club, then back and forth into the bunkers off and on all night with mortar fire. A couple of the guys that I had talked with at the EM Club were on their way back to the field for a second tour. Six more months, and they would both get an early out. Maybe I would try to stay a second tour and get out early.

The next day rolled around, and I still did not have my orders. Not that I was complaining, but most of the guys had received their orders and had flown out to join their units. That night at the EM Club, as I sat there drinking a brew, a guy burst through the doors and started shooting off an M16 rifle. We all hit the floor, and then he was jumped by Military Police while he was trying to reload. This was no training session. This guy flipped out! The police took him away. After all of the commotion, I went back to my hooch.

That night, I just could not sleep. Too much was going on. My mind was a whirl, and I was really getting scared.

Chapter 17

The following morning, I received my orders. I would be going to the 1st 327th 101st Airborne Division.

I would be leaving right away and flying up to Da Nang on the coast of the South China Sea, and then take a chopper from there to my unit. I would be working in the Highlands south of Hue, close to the DMZ, in the mountains. I wondered what had happened to the guy that I was replacing. Maybe it was best that I didn't know.

I was issued a rucksack with a full case of C rations and eight canteens of water, an M16 rifle, at least twenty pounds of ammo, some medical supplies, and an empty ammo can for my personal items, mail, etc.

I had to sit on the ground to put it on my back to lift it. When I got it on, I was hardly able to stand up because it was so heavy, but I was ready to go in minutes and board the chopper. I sort of waddled up the back plank, trying not to stumble with all of this weight on my back . . . Then off we went flying over the army base.

I could see the door gunners watching the ground closely for enemy activity.

It was a noisy helicopter, but I guess they all are. Moments later, we were at Bien Hoa Air Base and landing next to a large, old C140 aircraft.

After transferring from the chopper to the plane, I was strapped in against the wall of the plane sideways, and we began taxiing. The plane shook so badly that I thought it was going to fall apart.

Finally, we were airborne and on our way to Da Nang.

Wow, the country sure did look different from up above. I could see many pits where bombs had been dropped. What a shame. This country was so torn up.

I dozed off during the long flight. The vibrations sort of put me to sleep after a while.

Here it was, Da Nang, Vietnam, but I didn't get to see it, as I was off and on another chopper.

Now, we were flying over the coast and mountains. It was beautiful here, and it almost made one forget that there was a war going on.

We arrived at my new home base, a firebase named Camp Eagle south of Hue. I quickly walked off the plane and tried to stand straight, but it was difficult carrying my pack. I was met by my new first sergeant, Sergeant Ames, an old fat guy who smelled like beer. He instructed me to follow him to my tent for the night, as I would not be joining my unit until tomorrow morning.

I dropped off my rucksack as quickly as possible. I couldn't believe how heavy it was. He then took me around the camp and pointed out the mess hut and beer hut (both tents) and told me a little about where I was going.

The unit I would be joining worked as an eleven-man team—search-and-destroy missions. We followed orders that were called to us through our radio almost daily. Our mission was to guard different areas and/or locate Viet Cong in said areas. The unit came into live fire often and has had casualties. I was the only new person joining this team. I would be expected to do anything my sergeant told me to do and follow all orders. I was told that my sergeant, whom I would meet tomorrow, had been in Vietnam for about two years and had come close to being the only survivor in combat more than once.

Now, I was afraid—terrified, in fact! This was no longer fun.

Tomorrow, I would be joining a unit that was actually in combat.

I went to the beer hut and proceeded to have a few. I met some pretty interesting guys there who had just come out of the field for one reason or another. Some were leaving because it was the end of their tour (a tour is twelve months in Vietnam). Some were here for medical reasons. One guy was being sent out of the field for being crazy. He lost it during a firefight and almost got himself killed. They all had stories, and I listened engrossed as the night passed.

Morning came without any incoming mortars. It would have been a good night to sleep—except that I had so much on my mind—like staying alive.

I could not believe how heavy this rucksack was. I could hardly carry it. There was no way I could ever run or fight carrying such a heavy pack.

As the chopper arrived, I waddled up to it. I was about as ready as I could be. I was only hoping at this point that they didn't give me anything else to carry.

The helicopter ride was not long, only an hour or so. When we were in the air, I could again see the damage done on the ground by the bombs called in. We were landing in a mountainous area. I was terrified. How did I ever get myself into this?

I was told to get off the chopper. Not easy when you're carrying so much weight. I pulled myself off the chopper and walked about twenty feet to a clearing. As the helicopter flew off, I could see one man approaching me. He wore no shirt and wore a strap of ammo over his shoulder. He introduced himself.

"My name is Sergeant Henry."

"Hello, Sergeant," I replied.

He yelled, "Don't ever call me sergeant out here. You'll get me killed. Call me, Henry."

Henry stood about five foot ten with a thin build and spoke with a Southern accent. He had a somber face with no smile.

At the same time, another man walked up slowly. He was also not wearing a shirt, only straps of bullets, and hand grenades dangled from his body. He was a large, burly looking guy about six foot two and 250 pounds of muscle. He had scars all over his upper body from previous fights and/or bug bites. The longest was about eight inches down his left side. He walked up to me and said, "Where you from, punk?"

"California," I replied.

He laughed and then said, "How old are you?"

"Eighteen," I replied.

He then pulled off a hand grenade and said, "Have you ever killed anyone before?"

"No," I said and started to move a little backward as he was walking toward me with death in his eyes. He pulled the pin on the grenade and said, "Count it down, Cherry Boy."

I was terrified and counted out, "One Mississippi, two Mississippi, three Mississippi, four Mississippi," and he yelled out, "Grenade," and tossed it at me.

I was already stumbling backward from the weight of my pack, and I went over backward without catching the grenade. I landed on the ground, knowing I was dead!

Thankfully, it did not blow. I looked up then, realizing it was a dummy and heard him tell Sergeant Henry to "keep this fucking Cherry Boy away from me." Then he walked back into the brush.

Henry told me to get up. I had to take the rucksack off. I was now too weak to pick it up. I also noticed the heat. I was burning up, or at least I thought so.

Henry said, "What the hell are you carrying all of this crap for?"

I said, "This is what I was issued."

"Let me see what you have and what you really need."

He stripped it down to about one-third of what I was carrying and then called for the rest of the guys to come split up what I didn't need.

About ten men emerged out of the brush. The rest of the guys looked a little more normal. At least they were wearing shirts. None of them introduced themselves. I was definitely the youngest in the unit.

"This is Travis from California, and he'll be joining our group."

A few laughs and smirks, but nothing I couldn't live with. The guys immediately grabbed the extra canteens of water and C rations. This started a lunch and water break, which was good for me, as I felt so lost among these guys.

Henry came up to me and asked if I had ever fired an M79 grenade launcher. "Yes, I have but only once in training."

A few more laughs, and then Henry said, "Here, you're our new 'grenadier,'" as he handed me an M79 grenade launcher.

He then pointed at a tree on a mountaintop sticking up and said, "Now, hit that tree."

I pointed it up in the air and fired.

I didn't even hit the mountain. Instead of laughing, I heard things like, "Get rid of him," "OK, enough of him," "Send him back."

Henry commanded, "Fire again."

I loaded and fired again.

Again, I missed the mountain. Then we could hear the blast on the other side of the mountain. He said, "Raise your weapon higher and fire again."

I did it again and almost hit the tree right on target. I heard a few guys yell, "Yes, yes, all right," and Henry said, "You'll do."

He then gave me about sixty pounds of AG rounds to carry. I did not want to know what happened to the last guy who carried this, so I didn't ask.

Henry then took me aside and told me I would be working closely with him and to try my best to stay out of Crazy Charlie's way, because he didn't like me. Crazy Charlie was the guy who tossed me the fake grenade. He had now been here over two years, and he had truly gone crazy. He would rather stay out here and fight in live combat than to ever return home. I was told his wife finally gave up and divorced him.

I could see in Henry's eyes the respect that he held for Crazy Charlie, so I didn't say anything.

Later that day, Henry told me a little more about Crazy Charlie and the unit. Tears came to Henry's eyes when he said that twice in the past two years, they had been overrun, and all died except for Crazy Charlie and him. Both times, Crazy had lost his ammo bearer and had to make a stand. The .60 caliber weighed about twenty-eight pounds loaded. Both times, he stood and fired it from his hip. I could not imagine anyone shooting a .60 caliber from his hip, but then again, Crazy Charlie was not a typical soldier.

I was told we would be walking a lot, sleeping on the ground, and changing positions weekly or daily based on the calls from the radio with our instructions. We would be walking through the jungle and forests. I only had AG rounds and not Beehive that shoot like a large shotgun shell, so I had to be very careful when I fired the M79 as the AG rounds can go off by hitting a tree branch above. I needed to be in a clear space to fire. Thank God I would never walk "point" (first man) because I was carrying an M79. A point man must carry the M16.

Our point man was Terry from Georgia. He'd been here for six months and was planning on going home after his first year. He had a wife and child back home. His current rank was E4. He was drafted and had no plans to stay in the service.

Our radioman was Tony from New York. He was always on the radio with Command. He also had been here for about six months and had no plans of staying any longer. Tony's rank was also E4.

Our first day, we walked through the jungle for about three hours, moving very slowly as our point man, Terry, searched for mines and booby traps every step. This was really scary, knowing that any minute, the Viet Cong (Charlie) could jump out from behind a bush and start shooting. Night was drawing near, and Henry was planning on a spot to set up our "night perimeter" (sleep area and guard stations). This was no camping trip. We would be spreading out about twenty feet apart and taking turns sleeping and guard duty throughout the night.

There would be no fire that would alert the enemy and no noise or talking. We slept in two-hour shifts, two hours of sleep and two hours of guard duty. Sleeping up against a tree was not easy—one man on each side of the tree. I thought the night was going to last forever. The mosquitos never let up.

When morning finally came, I felt terrible. I hurt all over and had bug bites everywhere. We ate some of our C rations for breakfast. Of course, we had no fire to heat anything—what a horrible way to start the day.

Tony had been on the radio getting new instructions.

There was word of the North Vietnamese Army (NVA) moving through the jungle about five miles away from us. We were to find and stop them from moving any further south. We were in the mountains south of the city of Hue, which was a major crossing for the North Vietnamese Army.

We'd moved about three miles when Terry came back and informed Henry that there must be twenty NVA (North Vietnamese Army) ahead of us. Tony was already on the radio with Command and informed them.

We were told to stop the NVA, and if we got in trouble, call for fire support. The fear was growing among us. We all knew what could happen when eleven men took on twenty. We moved within one mile of where we thought the NVA were located. I remembered my training: "Kill, kill, kill!"

Then, to my surprise, I heard Tony on the radio to Command calling for fire support now. I heard Henry reading off grid coordinates for the bombing. We all got down, took cover, and waited. In just minutes, we could hear the whistle in the air of the 155 rockets slamming into the mountain in front of us.

Boom, boom, boom, the rockets pounded the mountains.

They were coming from US Navy ships. Then, we heard the helicopters buzzing overhead and the .50-caliber guns sounding off. Henry had us move forward. I could hear M16 fire and AK-47 fire, meaning Terry was probably right in the middle of them now. Henry had me fire the M79 over the mountain to the far side so that I would not hit any of our men but could hit any NVA trying to fall back. I could now hear Crazy Charlie firing his .60 caliber, and all our men opened fire.

Kill, kill, kill!

Then it stopped as fast as it had begun, with no sounds of any weapon fire at all. The helicopters were still buzzing overhead and moving more north as they were on the trail of any NVA trying to flee. Tony was on the radio, getting instructions to move.

Another chopper landed, and we all boarded to fly another forty klicks (a klick is 1,000 meters) north to stop the rest of the NVA group that had been spotted. None of our men were hit, but then again, by the time we got there, rockets had pounded the mountain. Henry said that next time; we were not going to get as close before we called for fire support. Night was approaching, so Henry had us set up a perimeter for the night. We would search for the NVA in the morning.

Once again, two-hour shifts of sleeping and two hours of guard duty. This was not easy to get used to, and the ground was not getting any softer. Despite this, I was so tired by my turn to sleep that I went into a deep sleep.

My eyes flew open with the sounds of bombing in the background that shook the earth.

I realized now why so many men were dying here. It was because we were hunting each other down like animals. I could not believe this was real. Tears came to my eyes as I thought of my chances of getting out of this alive. I wondered if I would ever see home and my mom and dad again.

It was early morning. We had a quick bite of cold C rations and moved out. Johnny, who walked the slack, or second position, told me our motto. "We are the 101st Airborne, the Screaming Eagles of Vietnam. War is our business, and Business has been good."

I really thought some of these guys were actually enjoying themselves. I could hear Crazy Charlie trying to convince Henry to move in even closer next time so that we could get in more action. Henry did not go for it. Good thing.

As we swept the mountain looking for the NVA, we noticed several tunnels. Our tunnel rat, Hobson, would inspect each one and then blow up the entrance with a hand grenade. It was like the NVA disappeared, but we knew they could be deep underground in the tunnels.

In the field, it's easy to lose track of days and time. After a few weeks, I felt that I had been here for months. At least, I had been more accepted by the men once they found out that I trained at Camp Crockett. Even Crazy Charlie spoke to me a little as he had a friend that went through Crockett.

Another operation was finally over. We went up and down canyons and waded streams for three days. The last day was rough, as no one had any rations left to eat. Also, the heat was just killing us. We only spotted a few VC very far away. I fired several 79 rounds but never knew if I hit anyone. The scouts said that none of the VC wanted to fight but left a few horrible Punji pits (traps with sharpened spikes often contaminated with urine or feces). Luckily for our guides, all pits were discovered, and none of us fell into one.

The village we entered was empty . . . a very strange feeling. The village smelled very bad, sort of a rotten smell. The VC knew we were coming. It is like all of the people just vanished.

Henry was talking with Command on what to do. We had no casualties, and the VC, for some reason, had disappeared from the area. To our surprise, Henry was told to get all of us ready to move out. We were getting three days at Eagle Beach, north of Hue, an in-country R&R center for the 101st Airborne. We were ready and picked up by chopper that afternoon.

Wow, my first night on a real cot since being in the field. What a difference. I slept so soundly in between waking up every two hours, thinking it was my turn for guard duty. What a nice treat: hot meals, cold beer, and a beach. Lots of guys here from the 101st, with all kinds of wild stories. One guy said it had now been a full month since he slept on a cot. Music played every night, and for a few moments, you could completely forget about the war.

Time went by fast. Soon, it was on to another operation.

CHAPTER 18

As we walked through the mountains, we crossed several creeks and filled our canteens when we could. That's why we only carry a couple each as we fill them up in mountain streams. We did not walk far when Henry announced that we had a chopper coming in with supplies and mail.

Wow, mail. I wondered if I would get a letter.

When the chopper landed, all the men were eagerly waiting—mail call.

Yes, I had a letter from home, from Mom and Dad.

Mom was doing fine. Dad was now walking five miles a day for his heart condition. I wondered if I would ever see him again. No other letters were for me and no letter from Gerri. I had not heard from her since I saw her in Oklahoma. I was starting to think that she must have found someone else, like Jody.

It got very quiet when the mail call was over. The men with letters were reading and in their own world of dreams. The men with no mail sat around with sad looks on their faces. Most all had letters to send home. I wrote Mom and Dad one, and another letter to Gerri. Mail was free for us to send.

Henry announced, "The dreams are over for the week. Prepare to move out."

We were going up another mountain searching for Viet Cong or NVA. The NVA use these mountains as a path from North Vietnam to the south. It seemed like more were coming through daily.

As we started moving up the mountain, the rain began to fall. I always thought I liked the rain . . . until now. We all put our letters in our individual ammo can to keep dry so that we could reread them later. The rain was now coming down so hard that we had to stop and find cover under the trees.

Henry sent two men ahead as scouts, and the rest of us spread out into a circular position. Henry was worried that we could be hit, as "Charlie," the Viet Cong, was known to take advantage of the rain. I was snuggled up to a tree, praying we would not be hit. I put my pack on the ground and stood ready to use my grenade launcher. It was cold, wet, and just plain miserable. And now, it was starting to get dark. Then we heard shots in the distance and a slow fire—one, two, three—a message for Henry to move us in.

Tony was on the radio with Command. They knew we were engaging enemy fire and needed grid quadrants for the bombing. Henry told Tony as soon as we located our scouts, we would give Command the grid quadrants. As we topped the mountain, we heard the shots go off again, signalling Henry their position. They seemed to be trapped about halfway up the next mountain. Henry told me, "This is your chance. I want you to cover the top of that mountain with 79 rounds."

As I started firing the M79, bullets began coming down the mountain. I was terrified, feeling that *I* was now the target. I had to be in the open to fire the M79 so as not to hit any branches above me. I fired as fast as I could. Henry had sent some men to the bottom of the mountain, and I could hear both M16 fire and AK-47 fire. I must have shot ten rounds to the top of the mountain, and I heard Crazy Charlie sounding off with his .60 caliber.

It was very difficult to explain the feeling you have in a firefight. The adrenalin rushed so hard, and everything seemed to move so fast but yet in slow motion. It was very weird.

Our men at the bottom of the hill started to pull back, both scouts with them. Henry said, "Now, fall back about one mile," and he had Tony call Command for fire support to bomb the mountain.

Henry said to me, "Good job with that 79." He was not the kind of person to give out compliments. That felt so good.

It was getting darker by the minute, and I was so scared to go through the forest.

Then, *boom, boom, boom.* We could hear the navy 122 and 155 rockets coming in and hitting the mountain. They were so powerful that the ground shook when they hit. Henry was yelling on the radio, "I want more!"

The entire sky lit up with tracers coming from both directions. Choppers surrounded the mountain. Beehive rockets, .50 calibers . . . The entire mountain was in flames.

Soon after the mountain lit up, Henry announced on the radio that all men were now safe, and we would drop back about another mile and set up a night perimeter. It was so dark by the time we stopped we could hardly see the trees in front of us. Each man sat up against a tree for shelter and protection. As usual, we would all do two-hour shifts of sleeping and guard duty. It was hard to sleep. I was so wet and cold. I calmed down as it became quiet, and my mind drifted off to home.

Daylight again, and Henry and Tony had been busy on the radio. The rain was letting up, and if the sun came out, at least we could dry off.

Move out!

It was time again. We were moving closer to the mountain again, or at least what was left of it. Choppers were buzzing around the mountain, but no shots were fired. We were now on top of the next mountain from where I was shooting the 79. Henry received word on the radio that the mountain was now secure, and we were to drop back.

The NVA had been cut off on the other side of the mountains by another unit. We would not have to sweep this mountain or chase them. I was so relieved. But I wondered what we would face next.

The next day was great, with lots of sunshine to dry us out and nobody shooting at us. We all ate our lunch rations and talked about home and family. I didn't realize that some of these guys even had a family. Some liked to talk about their girls and share all of their intimate details. Some talked about their high school days. Crazy Charlie was quiet and said very little.

Tony was on the radio with Command early the next morning. Good thing Henry called in for such heavy air support as they did turn out to be NVA. We could have easily been overrun. I realized that just one bad mission . . . and it could all be over.

We would not get orders to move to a new location until the following day. This gave us a whole day to read our mail, enjoy the sun, and even take turns bathing in a small stream with cold but very refreshing water.

The next morning came with Tony on the radio with Command. The choppers were on the way. Henry got back on the radio with Command himself to discuss our new mission. He didn't like it.

It didn't take long for the choppers to arrive. We quickly loaded up, and off we went. Flying over jungle and mountains in a chopper was scary because there were so many snipers firing at the choppers. But nobody fired at us this time—what a relief.

When we landed at the base of a large mountain, we were all shocked to see how much metal was on the ground from shrapnel and spent cartridges. The ground was literally covered. It was hard to see the dirt. Henry was worried. He said we were not going up the mountain today. He wanted to stay at the bottom and send up scouts first. He spent most of the day on the radio, and what he found out was not pleasant.

The mountain was called Bac Mao. At the top was a French resort from many years ago. Now, it is a Viet Cong stronghold that could not be bombed for religious reasons. The swimming pools at the resort were now sealed up bunkers. The Viet Cong fired mortars from there down the mountain. We found a large rock, and written on it was: *US Marine Corps*, but we could not read what division. Henry said this was where all the fragments and spent shells came from. The marines had tried to take Bac Mao at one time. Henry and Crazy Charlie walked away together so they could talk without the rest of us hearing them. I could hear Charlie saying, "Let me take my 60 up the mountain and find out how fucking bad they really are."

I flashed back on my childhood of deer hunting. Day in and day out during the season, we would hunt deer. Now, we are hunting men.

I was really wondering why we are all here hunting each other like it's a big game. Henry had also sent scouts out around the base of the mountain, and what they found was a little more pleasant. They had found a "soda boy" who said he would bring us warm beer and girls from the village.

In the late afternoon, our scouts returned, saying it would be impossible to get to the top of the mountain. It became so steep we would need climbing gear to make it. Also, we would become perfect targets because most of the growth had been burned.

The soda boy did show up with three girls and some warm local rice beer known as Ba Muoi Ba or 33 beer. I can't believe how good warm beer really tastes at a time like this. The girls were not very good looking. They looked like they lived a very hard life. They did not speak any English, but the soda boy spoke a little. He said the girls wanted two dollars MPC (Military Payment Certificate) each for a "short time" (a "short time" is a quick lay). About half of the guys were interested and walked off into the brush with the girls. I was shocked. I had never seen anything like this in my life. When they came back, the girls seemed very pleased with the money they made. I figured the girls made about ten dollars US each, which is a lot of money to them, but how gross!

I got the chance to use my Vietnamese that I had been learning from the small book that I bought when I first came into the country.

I tried to practice the language to myself a little bit every day.

To my surprise, my Vietnamese was pretty good. We learned that we are not in a safe place because as soon as the Viet Cong realized we were at the bottom of the mountain, they would fire mortars at us.

We were invited to stay in their village. They claimed it was not Viet Cong. Henry said we would accept the offer, but we would remain on the village outskirts, just in case. We took what warm beer we had left and followed them to their village about five miles away. Henry, Charlie, and Terry walked with the soda boy and girls into the village to meet with their village leader. We were all spread out and ready to open fire if necessary. When they returned, they said it appeared to be safe, and we would set up our night perimeter on the outskirts. From where we set up for the night, we could smell the stench of the village. There are no bathrooms or running water, a scene that would be fitting for a *National Geographic* magazine article. It was hard to believe that people lived like this.

We slept for two hours on and two hours off, as usual. It was a warm and balmy night, but I slept well just knowing we were close to some sort of civilization.

The next morning, Henry was busy with Tony on the radio, telling Command that we were working our way around and slowly up the mountain. He then told us that we were going to spend the day by the village water supply, swimming and enjoying life.

I didn't believe it. He *was* human. I had been starting to wonder.

All the men were relieved to find out that Henry had no plans to take on the mountain. He said we would play with Command as long as he thought we could get away with it.

The day was wonderful. We all bathed in the river, told stories of home, and for the first time, I started to get to know some of the guys. To my surprise, two of the guys went through Camp Crockett but would not talk about it. Henry did send out scouts throughout the day, and we did take turns, as usual, on guard duty.

One of the girls came up and said the high priest would like us to join him for some Nuocc Mau, a rice dish with dried fish it in. Nobody wanted any, and most of our men made ugly faces or remarks. I said I would like to try it, and a few guys laughed. All of the village people came out of their huts to look at me.

The high priest was squatting on the ground with several other men and women, all with wooden bowls of rice that smelled like it came out of a septic tank. They all smiled to welcome me. Many of them were missing teeth or had very black ones with betel quid (betel nut) stains. Betel nut grows naturally in Vietnam and was chewed for the buzz, or high. (I never met an American that would chew betel nut.)

I squatted down with them and was passed a bowl of Nuocc Mau. On the first bite, I thought my stomach was going to turn over. I knew then that I had to do this. Why? I did not know, but I had to eat this with them. It was very difficult to swallow something that smelled so bad.

Once I realized that I could hold it down, I smiled to let them know I liked it. After I finished my bowl, a girl tried to give me more, but I rubbed my stomach to show her that I was full. I then said in Vietnamese, "I study from a book, and I understand a little." I could tell they all liked that, even though they were all speaking so fast that I really couldn't understand them. Suddenly, everyone fell silent and turned their attention to the high priest who began to speak. Very slowly, so that I could understand, he said, "All I want for my village is peace. We only have a little rice to live on. For many years, our rice paddies have been burned, our women have been raped, and our young men have been killed. Our village has been destroyed numerous times, and we always rebuild with what little we have left. I only ask you, please do not destroy our village."

I told him, "No, no, we are not here to destroy but to help make sure that it never happens again."

He looked at me closely with his rummy eyes and said that if the Viet Cong discovered that he allowed us to camp by their village, they would kill him, and that there could be Viet Cong right here in the village because they mix in with civilians.

A shiver went down my spine at *that* thought.

As I walked to join the other guys, Henry was ready to move out. Thinking I had knowledge to help, I told him what the high priest said about the Viet Cong, but his experience meant that he was already aware that the VC could have infiltrated the villagers.

During my absence, he had been on the radio with Tony, telling Command about our journey up the mountain. We were going about five miles the other way to a creek the soda boy had told him about where we would meet our chopper for supplies and mail in a few days. We set off, and as we walked, I started thinking of home again.

Would I get a letter from Gerri this time? Also, I wondered if Kenny had entered Vietnam yet.

After several days doing patrols in the area, we had not encountered the Viet Cong. Our soda boy had been meeting us almost daily with warm beer and girls. Now, we were trading cigarettes. We got two cartons each free every month. No wonder everybody here smoked.

It was mail call again, and we were all waiting patiently for our name to be called. Yes, I had mail and more than one. I had a letter from Mom and Dad and one from Gerri. I was so excited that I wanted to save hers for last.

Mom and Dad were both doing fine. They wrote that Kenny was at home again and would be leaving for Vietnam in a few days. Wow, I wondered if there was any way I might be able to see him in when he arrived.

Next, my heart racing with anticipation, I opened the letter from Gerri. It smelled like the scent she wore, and I inhaled the perfume deeply as I began to read it.

Dearest Ike,

I want to start by saying how much I enjoyed your visit here in Oklahoma. In just a few days, I was falling in love with you! I know in my heart that you will live through Vietnam. Now, I must ask you one thing. Please stop writing to me, and please do not ask me why. I will never see you again, but I wish you the best in life, as I know you deserve. I do not want you to think back on us. I only want you to concentrate on your future and living through Vietnam. This is goodbye, and if you really care for me, you will do as I ask and never write to me again.

Gerri

I was choking up. I had to walk off alone, but it was obvious to everyone that something had upset me. As I gazed at the huge bomb craters at the foot of Bac Mao in the distance, a strange feeling came over me, and for the first time, I was not afraid to die. In fact, I was no longer afraid of any of these guys either, so if any of them had any smart remarks to make, they would see a new side of me. Tears stopped, and anger set in.

Henry approached.

"It was from your girl back home, wasn't it?"

"Yes."

"Jody?"

"Yes."

He said the same thing had happened to him and half of the guys here. The best thing to do was to forget her and move on. As we walked up to the rest of the men, Tony just said, "Jody?"

And I said, "Yes."

None of the men gave me a hard time, and some swore at Jody. I heard one say, "Better to learn about the bitch now than later." They were right. I would go on with my life, and I would never write to her again.

Henry was on the radio again; telling Command there was no way to get to the top of the mountain. "If we can't bomb that mountain, we will never take it."

After about an hour, Command called with instructions to stay where we were for the rest of the day, and we would be picked up the following morning by chopper for our next mission.

CHAPTER 19

I HAD NOW been in Vietnam for over two months and was still alive. I continued to hate the fact that we never knew where we were going or what to expect, and Henry warned that we all needed to be very careful, as we had gone months without losing a man. The last man was the grenadier, killed a month before my arrival. Our luck could change at any time, and our days could be numbered.

It was time for the chopper to meet us with our weekly supplies and mail. I was always looking forward to my letters from home, and they arrived almost weekly from sisters, nieces, friends or Mom and Dad. I was also getting letters from a girl called Cathy, who my dad met in Chico, and he gave her my address. She was attending Chico State and looked good in her pictures. Maybe I'd see her when I got home. My sister Nadine had written a poem, which was published in our local newspaper, *The Live Oak Acorn*, and Mom sent me a copy.

A Brother Missed

No one can love her brother more than I
Oh, how I hope my brother does not cry
I miss his face, the talk, and the smile
It won't be long, just a while
One day he was in diapers, next on a bike
Into everything, and I screamed, Ike!
He was small as a boy and big as a man
And no one could be prouder of him than I am
Now he has gone off to war to fight for us here
I know it took courage not to show fear
And he is loved very much by his family and I
It took strength when he left for us not to cry
But the days will go by and time will soon pass
And before I know it, my brother will be home at last

As we prepared to move out, I put the letters in my ammo can to read again later in the week as most all of us do.

The weather was humid and not easy to walk in. When it's not raining, it's humid. Seems like we just can't win. We were in the mountains walking down into a canyon when I heard the water running. I reached for my canteens to see if I needed to fill them. I was still carrying two canteens, although some of the guys now only carried one. As I was filling them up, I heard Henry yell, "Don't drink the water. It looks bad."

Honestly, it didn't look good, but I thought of the odds of risking it against going without water in the heat, so I filled my canteens. As night approached, we were informed from our scouts that we were in a fairly safe area for the night. We set up in pairs and spread out among the trees. As usual, we worked shifts, two hours of guard duty, two hours of sleep. My partner, a guy named Joe from Dallas and whom I hardly knew as he never talked, nudged me awake, and I reached for my canteens. It was so humid and muggy, and I needed a drink. To my surprise, one canteen was empty. I was shocked.

What had happened? Who could have taken my water? Of course, it had to be Joe on the other side of the tree. I whispered to him, but he denied it and told me that I should know that we couldn't speak after dark.

The following morning, I told Henry about it, but he just said forget about it and move on.

That day, we walked and walked for miles without seeing another human being. Late in the day, Joe became very sick. He started vomiting heavily and accused me of poisoning him with my water—the same water he had denied stealing. All the guys began to look at me as if I tried to kill Joe by "allowing" him to steal my water.

Joe (the oldest guy in the unit at twenty-nine) became so ill that Henry had to call for a helicopter to medevac him out.

I explained to Henry about the water being from the stream that had looked bad, but I had some, and I felt fine. The other guys continued to cast accusing glances at me, and Henry told me for the sake of my life, he better not find out that I poisoned Joe.

That night, nobody wanted to partner up with me for guard duty, and I was terrified that if we got into a firefight that the .60 caliber might be turned on me.

It was a sleepless night, but I was still not feeling any adverse effects from the supposed contaminated water. As daylight approached, however, I started feeling very sick and having very sharp stomach pains. I told Henry about it but received no sympathy. Just told to forget about it and move on. Hard to forget about it when you are feeling ill.

Within an hour, I started vomiting and could not stop. I became so weak, I could not stand up. I was so sick. I told Henry to go ahead and move out and just let me lie here and die. I felt that bad.

I was so feverish I became delusional and begged for it to be over. My thoughts turned to home, and I could feel the love of my mom reaching out for me. I prayed to die soon and not be caught by the Viet Cong. I could hear gunshots but had no idea who was shooting.

I must have passed out because I woke up in a helicopter with a medic putting a needle in my arm.

I was alive! I could not believe it.

I fell back asleep.

When I woke again, I learned that I was in the 8th Medevac Field Hospital, Vietnam. The medics thought I had malaria, and they would start treating me now, but we would not get the results back for six or seven days. Strangely, I had bruises all over my body. It was as if I had been beaten up, but I had no memory of what caused them. I had no idea what happened to me. I didn't know if we were in a firefight or what?

The hospital consisted of several tents. Many of the patients here had horrific injuries, and I saw many removed with sheets over their heads. A real awakening of the war! Up to now, I hadn't noticed how horrific this war was, but soldiers were dying here daily, and the wounded were constantly arriving. It was the most distressing place I had ever seen in my life.

I would sleep most of the day, but when I did wake, I thought about my unit, how lucky we had been up to now, and wondered how long we would survive before we got blown away.

I dreamed of home, my parents, my sisters, and all of my friends that I might never see again.

After several days, I was told that I did not have malaria, and they did not know what I had, so I was being transported to Na Trang for better care at a real hospital. I was flown out by helicopter later that day for Na Trang Hospital.

After about a week in Na Trang, the doctors gave up and said they had no idea what was wrong with me. By this time, my blood pressure and fever had reduced, but I was getting sharp stomach cramps and pain. However, because they couldn't tell what was causing the problem, they decided to send me back to my unit, even though the stomach cramps continued daily.

A chopper flew me to Camp Eagle, where I reported to my rear unit and was told I would be flying out to join up with my company in the field tomorrow morning.

Chapter 20

BACK AT THE tent where I was staying for the night, I met a guy named Darrell, who, I discovered, was a trained mechanic. He was very excited because he was getting ready to leave for his new duty station. He was going to be deployed in the motor pool and would not be going back to the field. I asked him how he had managed this, and he explained that he just asked the first sergeant how he could transfer as a mechanic and was told that they needed one with his skills right away.

Wow, I thought, *how lucky is that*. He then told me that the first sergeant had said what they really needed was someone who could teach typing. This was *my* chance. *I* could teach typing.

I immediately ran down to the first sergeant's tent and asked if there was a need for a typing instructor. Sure enough, he said yes. After looking at my records, he informed me that there was a great need for a typing instructor, but he would need to be a Sergeant.

He explained that last year in the Tet Offensive of '68, we lost so many men from the 101st Airborne that the clerks were pulled out into the field. Most were never replaced, and now they needed an instructor to teach typing—and soon. Due to transfers in and out of Camp Eagle, now, thousands of orders were backed up.

I convinced him that I could do it, but I would first have to compete against others in a timed typing test. He called Bien Hoa Command to explain the situation and later came to my tent to tell me to get ready to leave in the morning for Bien Hoa. There, I would be tested, and if I were good enough, I would get a "field grade promotion" as a Sergeant of a Personnel Service Center, teaching typing, cutting orders, etc. I couldn't believe my good fortune. If I got the job, I would be promoted to an E4 right away, and within three months, be a Sergeant E5.

I was so excited. I decided to stop by the Mess Tent for a cold beer and met more guys coming and going to the field. I hardly slept that night, thinking I might not be returning to the field, but the sound of gunfire in the distance didn't help, either.

The following morning, I went to the first sergeant's tent for my orders. The game had now changed somewhat. He informed me that because I was only a Private E3, I would need to reenlist in the army for eight months for me to have the post. I began to argue with him, but he simply told me if I did not like it, I could go back out in the field. He then gave me handwritten orders to hand in to Bien Hoa should I choose to go. Looking at my options, I quickly decided that it would be worth spending another eight months in the army just to sleep on a real cot.

I prayed as we flew to Bien Hoa, thanking God for this opportunity. This time, I could see out a window, and as I gazed out, I thought to myself what a beautiful country Vietnam really is . . . if you take the war part out of it.

As I walked into the Quonset hut where I would be taking the typing test, I worried about my competition. I could tell by the new clothes and boots they all just arrived from the "world." The world is what we call the United States or "back home." These guys have probably all used typewriters recently and would have a great edge over me because I had not touched one in over a year.

The officer in charge of the test, a captain, told us to take a blank piece of paper, put it into our typewriters, and prepare for the test. We would be using the AR Regulations book and had five minutes to type without any errors.

He informed us that he would be choosing a new sergeant to teach typing and speed up the delivery of orders.

I boldly spoke up. "Sir, shouldn't we all have one minute to practice the alphabet before the test, as we should all be aware of any keys that might stick?"

It was true that we needed to know what keys might stick, but more importantly, I wanted a minute to practice the alphabet and get my hands "back."

He agreed.

"I will grant one minute to practice. Then we will change paper and begin the test. One minute starts now."

As I slowly started typing the alphabet, I flashed back on the many times I had been in speed typing tests. I told myself, "I can do this, and I know it."

As the minute passed, my hands became faster and faster.

The officer called, "Time. Change paper and turn to page 387 and begin. You have five minutes."

I was getting nervous, and I knew that was when you made mistakes. I was typing for my life, and I knew it. Oh no, about halfway through the page, I made a mistake. Hesitating, looking at my error for a moment, my eyes got watery as I flashed on the guys out in the field, and I realized that I could be one of them again if I failed this test. I went forward typing as fast as I possibly could. The fear had left me, as I knew that I had already made a mistake. I couldn't do anything about that now, but I could still finish first.

Finally, I was done. I pulled out my paper and said, "Sir, I am sorry, but I have one error in the middle of the page."

He looked up at me in amazement and said, "You're finished?"

I said, "Yes, sir."

THE OTHER SIDE OF NAM

He asked if anyone else was finished. "No," they said. They were still typing. The officer and I stared at each other for a moment, and then he said to everyone, "Stop your typing."

Once again, he asked if anyone else had finished, and to my surprise, nobody else had. In fact, they were not even halfway through the page. He then looked at me and said, "Congratulations. You are really fast. I just hope that you can teach your men to type like that. You are now an acting Sergeant E5, although you will still need to go in front of the E5 board, but that will be automatic."

"Do you want to train these men, or should I send them to the field?" he asked.

All my former competitors begged me, "Please take me. I really can type." I knew none of them wanted to go out in the field, so I thought, why not? I would have to teach someone. All seemed to speak up at the same time thanking me.

"Yes," I said, "I will teach them."

CHAPTER 21

Wow, now, I was an acting sergeant. I would wear the sergeant stripes and acquire the duties, even though I would not be officially promoted for a couple of months. I could not believe it. I get to work at Bien Hoa Army Base and would not be going back into the field!

That night, I met with the major and a couple of other officers, and we discussed my duties as a new sergeant of the Personnel Service Center. I would now have my own Quonset hut office and have about 20 men working with me.

We were really backed up in work, as there were boxes and boxes of orders for promotions, citations, leaves, etc. that needed to be posted.

My first task as a personnel sergeant was to teach the men to type to an acceptable standard as quickly as possible. I had them practice all day until they could all do thirty words per minute, and after just a few days, I gave them timed tests just like in high school. It was amazing how quickly they learned. During that time, we spent the evening posting orders, awards, etc. to their corresponding records in an attempt to clear the backlog.

We slept in a hooch (a Quonset hut), which was divided into sections with blankets for about sixteen of us to give a little bit of privacy. I got lucky and ended up with a corner spot next to the door.

The guys in my hooch and in my office were from various states back in the "world" and all walks of life. Living in the "rear," as it was called in a combat zone, was totally different from living in the field, fighting, eating C rations, and sleeping on the ground.

In the rear, you had a life with hot meals, clean clothes, water, and a fun nightlife in an NCO Club (non-commissioned officers), with Vietnamese singers almost every night.

It did not take me long to adjust to this kind of life, even though we were awake many nights sitting in a bunker with mortars flying over our heads.

After my first week as personnel sergeant, a captain took me around and introduced me to several officers with instructions to do whatever these guys wanted. I was also introduced to a payroll sergeant and told that I would be working closely with him.

Despite my improved circumstances, I was still suffering occasional sharp stomach pains and just knew that something wasn't right. The company medic insisted that he couldn't find anything wrong.

My first week as I was delivering orders to Long Binh, I heard my name called: Ike! To my surprise it was Rusty Andreason from Live Oak. He was the Principals son and just coming into Vietnam. Rusty was one year ahead of me in school but for that one moment it was like we were best of friends. It was great to see him!

As part of my duties, I was also listed as a sergeant of the guard, meaning that once a week, I was in charge of the bunkers surrounding our unit for 24 hours. These bunkers were lined up all around the base, and as sergeant of the guard, or berm sergeant, it was my duty to patrol each bunker, making sure that all the guards were awake and alert. I was always pleased to report everything was OK.

Chapter 22

I QUICKLY BEGAN to make friends with everyone in the unit. I also had an education in life I had never encountered before. Most of the guys and officers were doing some kind of drugs . . . pot, opium, liquid speed. It was all available.

I'd never done anything like this and couldn't understand how they could either.

Changing money on the black market was also a big thing, and almost everyone was doubling money upon the exchange. It seemed all you had to do was give your mama-san (Vietnamese lady who cleans the hooch and does the laundry) some US currency, and she would exchange it into MPC (Military Payment Certificate) and give you back twice as much the next day. I heard that before I got here, they were paying up to four times as much, and guys were making fortunes. Also, I learned that everything was for sale on the black market, including military Jeeps, which occasionally disappeared from our unit.

As the weeks passed, I would get instructions to change orders for certain guys (usually officers), sometimes the date of entry into

Vietnam, to make their tour actually shorter, or sometimes changing or eliminating the dates of an R&R (rest and relaxation). To make this work, I had to get to know one person in payroll, as our records had to match. If an R&R had been eliminated from the personnel records and the payroll records, then the guy would still have an R&R due him. It was usually a case where an officer would spend one R&R in Hawaii with his wife, and then a few months later, take another R&R with some other officers to play in Hong Kong or Singapore. I never thought about it being right or wrong. I just followed my orders.

Soon, I heard that one of the guys in our unit was going back to the "world," as his tour was over, and he would not come back. Naturally, he was looking forward to going home but was complaining because he was still only twenty years old and could not even buy a beer when he got back—even after serving his country in a war zone.

Well, after giving it some thought, I told him that I could change the birth date on ID cards as I'd done it in the past and suggested he give me his. That evening, I faultlessly altered his birth date and replaced the laminate so that no one could detect the alteration. Word spread like wildfire throughout the unit, and the next day, I got a request from one of the officers in payroll to change several more. I quickly became very popular and started to receive invites and favors.

I received an invite to go with some of the guys to Saigon and party for a couple of days. Some of the guys would even sneak out after dark to Bien Hoa, a Viet Cong-controlled village, and I was invited to go along. Once you got there, you would find a "party house" with girls, warm beer, and Dinky Dau Tuock (pot-rolled cigarettes), and I have even been invited to the evening smoke out. I knew this was happening every night, but I did not pay any attention to it as I was always in the NCO Club listening to music and had never had any interest in the drug scene.

The smoke out is where all of the pot smokers met every night in front of the Quonset huts and smoked together. The pot was placed in a large bowl, and several tubes like hoses called hookahs came out of it that people smoked through.

Well, I'd never done this before but decided to give it a try. After all, it couldn't be too bad for you as so many guys were doing it. When the hookah hose was passed to me, I inhaled slightly and held it like all of the other guys were doing. Then I started to get light-headed and realized that I must be getting "stoned," as they called it.

As we smoked, we exchanged stories about our lives back in the world, and then the jokes started, and I had never laughed so hard in my life. We had a great night, and I slept like a log, only getting up one time to run for the bunker with the sound of an alarm.

As time went by, my job began to change a little, and I started flying with officers all over Vietnam with orders for various units. We would stay in fun party places like Saigon, Vũng Tàu, Cam Ranh Bay, etc. Wow, was my life changing.

I was now also the Platoon Leader and responsible for all of the men being present for "platoon check" early each morning. Not all of the men showed up for platoon check for one reason or another, but as long as I knew where they were, I usually checked them off. A couple of the guys were usually on Perimeter Berm Guard Duty, and sometimes a few would decide to sneak into Bien Hoa village for the night.

Since changing units, I hadn't received my mail from home, but it had finally caught up to me, and it included a box of cookies from Mom. I quickly began to write my replies, and it sure was easier to answer letters when you had a typewriter handy.

Chapter 23

I was getting used to "hot food" again. I used to think the food in a mess hall was terrible, but after eating C rations in the field, mess halls were like gourmet. The sight leaving the mess hall after meals, however, was distressing as old Vietnamese people lined up with garbage cans for you to clean your tray into. They took these cans back to their village to feed their families. The cans were pretty gross with all of the cigarette butts the guys snuffed out in their trays after eating. There were no welfare programs at all to help the Vietnamese people, and many were starving. It was very sad to see.

Almost every night, mortars bombarded the camp, sending us all running to our bunkers. Many times, mortars hit Bien Hoa Army Base that was intended for the air base but fell short. Either way, it was terrifying knowing if one landed close to you; it was "all over." The night sky lit up when these mortars came in with all of the lights on the base and helicopters and gunships in the air looking for the Viet Cong. We could usually hear the firefight when they were finally spotted. Then, just as fast as it all started, it got quiet. This was nighttime at Bien Hoa

Army Base. It was always such a pleasure when you slept through the night without being woken up with mortars. Sometimes, you would even sleep through with mortars coming in, and you wouldn't know it until the next morning. This happened to most of the soldiers living at Bien Hoa Army Base.

I still get sharp, stabbing pains in my stomach almost every day, but other than that, I felt good and was very pleased to be out of the field.

Some of the guys asked me to go with them to Saigon for the weekend. We would make Friday our day of delivery for orders to be taken to Long Binh Army Base, which was on the way to Saigon. That way, we could drop off the orders and have a Jeep with a driver to take us to Saigon afterward.

As we left the gate at Bien Hoa Army Base, the guard looked at our orders and said, "So, it takes four men to deliver these orders now?" and laughed.

I was a little uneasy in the Jeep because you never knew when a sniper might attack, but we made the hour-plus drive from Bien Hoa Army Base to Saigon without incident. One of the guys, Roy, pointed out the "drop-off" spot for the nighttime trip to Bien Hoa village, where I planned to go one night. He also explained how you would need to hide from both the US Cobra gunships and Viet Cong while sneaking into the village at night to party.

This guy Roy came from a fairly wealthy family in Ohio. He had a very interesting life, and he took a lot of chances. This was his third tour in Vietnam, and I wondered if maybe he had been here too long. Also with us was Jerry from New Jersey who seemed to have grown up in a very wild area and had taken all kinds of drugs in his life. The fourth guy, Jimmy, was our driver. He was from Texas and, as a child, had lived a very sheltered life. Jimmy was "right off the ranch" and seemed to know more about animals than he did people.

The drive to Saigon was exciting, and Saigon was unreal. There were thousands of bicycles, small cars, lambrettas, carts with people pulling them, military Jeeps, large military trucks, and people all frantically walking around the streets. I had never imagined such congested streets with thousands of people all at once. What a crowd to get through, and everybody moved at once.

The stench was horrible, especially with the heat. Between the stink of the city and the exhaust fumes, I was getting a little sick. Finally, we were at the Milan Hotel, an old run-down hotel with a very wild bar full of GIs and Saigon Tea Girls. This is where you could buy a girl some Saigon Tea, and she would be your company or date while you enjoyed beer and good laughs with all of the guys. No more tea, no more girl. She would move on to another GI if you did not keep buying her Saigon Tea.

A room for the night cost US four dollars or a carton of cigarettes, either Salem or Pall Mall. Many of us carried a couple of cartons as "currency" because they were free in our unit, and we could hold on to our dollars.

The beer that we drank was called Ba Moui Ba and left one of the worst hangovers ever imagined. After partying and drinking this beer for two days, I was ready to go back to the base. Wow, I met so many GIs over the weekend that had sneaked off from their units to be able to party, I wondered with all of the GIs in Saigon, who was left fighting the war?

CHAPTER 24

ONE GI I knew still fighting was my cousin, Kenny. I received a letter last week from Mom saying that Kenny was in Vietnam with the 82nd Airborne, working down in the Delta, out in the field as a grunt infantryman. I could not imagine the life he must be living, but I certainly had not forgotten how terrible it was out fighting in the field. Poor Kenny. I hoped that he makes it, and I wondered if I would ever see him in Vietnam?

The ride back to Bien Hoa Army Base was a little quieter than the trip to Saigon. All four of us could use some rest. Jerry thought that he had food poisoning and wanted to see the medic as soon as we got back. Me, I had stayed with the seafood, which I thought was great. The sight alone of the chicken always grossed me out, because they pick and hang them outside, where flies always cover them. If anything made Jerry sick, it was the chicken. I still had this constant stomach pain, but it was the same one I've had for a while (and the base doctor found nothing wrong with me).

It was almost dark when we arrived back at Bien Hoa Army Base.

It felt good to be back and safe on base. We could hear the live music playing at the NCO Club, but I was too tired to go in and listen.

Oh no! As soon as I lay down to sleep, the sirens started screaming, summoning us to go to our bunkers immediately as we had "incoming." Mortars were being fired into the base. I ran out so quickly that I was carrying my clothes with me. The night sky lit up right away, and I could hear the gunships in the air. This time, it seemed like forever as most of the night was spent in the bunker. The gunships could not pinpoint where the mortars were coming from. With the morning light, all became silent, and we went back to our bunks for a couple of hours of sleep before we started our day. Meanwhile, the infantry was sweeping the area by foot all around the base to make sure that we were secure.

At work in my Quonset hut office, all of the guys were asking questions about my trip to Saigon and asking if I ever planned on going into Bien Hoa village, even though it was Viet Cong controlled. Most of the guys had been to Saigon, but only a few had ventured into Bien Hoa village. I said, "Maybe another time."

During the week, I was informed that I would be flying to Nha Trang for the weekend with a couple of officers to deliver orders. Yes, *this* could be fun. Nha Trang was an old coastal city with a beautiful beach. I knew about the place because I was there at the hospital, but I did not get to venture out.

My men were jealous as I gathered the order changes, etc. that I needed for the trip.

The flight was exciting but still scary, as you never knew when bullets might start hitting the chopper. I was uncomfortable as I again had the same sharp stomach pains, which had been bothering me, and they persisted the entire flight.

Nha Trang was bustling with business, at least from what I could see. I was told to deliver the orders and where to meet in two days to fly back to Bien Hoa. Wow, other than delivering the orders, I was pretty much free for the next couple of days. I quickly found out where to stay on base and where the food and entertainment could be found.

Two days was not long enough. I met some of the nicest people on this base and totally enjoyed myself. The personnel sergeant, Andy, was great with me. After delivering the orders, he took me for a ride off the base. The coastline was amazing. Nha Trang was absolutely gorgeous! The bars were fun, and the music that was playing was American songs. This was a safe area, but you always needed to be on guard. Sometimes, it did get hit with mortars, but not while I was there.

The flight back was uneventful. The officers with me did not have much to say, and I enjoyed the flight. The trip had been like a mini vacation for me.

As we got closer to Bien Hoa, one of the officers announced that Bien Hoa was hit all night with mortars.

Welcome home, welcome to Bien Hoa.

Chapter 25

The months flew by. I was starting to feel like an old-timer, and I had even been to Bien Hoa village several times, partying with the Vietnamese girls.

There truly was another side of living in Vietnam other than out in the field, and I was actually living it. I had met guys now that have been over here for three years, and some of them were very happy. The motor pool sergeant was married to a Vietnamese girl and planned on returning to Vietnam after he got out of the service.

I occasionally wondered if I would still be alive had I stayed out in the field, and during these times, I also thought about Kenny. He had now been in Vietnam and out in the field for months. Mom talked to Aunt Nora (Kenny's mother) almost every week, so I knew that he was still surviving but that he had it really rough over here. I thought about him when it rained. When it rained in Vietnam, it really rained hard. The monsoons were unbelievable. At least we had a Quonset hut that protected us from the storms. I wondered what it was like where Kenny is right now?

The weekend was almost here, and some of the guys wanted to sneak into Bien Hoa village for the night, so I had tweaked the orders so we could leave right after dark.

As we passed through the gates at Bien Hoa Base, I handed the guard the orders to get us all off base, feeling a little nervous as I always did when I handed these out.

A few miles from Bien Hoa Army Base, the Jeep slowed down to a crawl. We all jumped off, as it was still moving so that if anyone were watching the lights, they wouldn't know that we got off. I rolled when I hit the ground to soften the impact, but it still hurt. We now needed to cross the field of rice with the American patrol planes flying over our heads. When we saw their lights coming at us, we lay still on the ground, and as soon as they passed over, we got up and ran again until the planes turned around and came back over us. It was about a mile run across the field.

As we made it, we saw the girls waiting with anticipation to see if they would receive any visit from GIs tonight. The girls welcomed us and guided us to the "Party House," where we could enjoy their company, drink warm beer, and feel relatively safe as the mama-san (the woman in charge) claimed that she paid off the Viet Cong "not to attack the house."

There were about five GIs and maybe ten girls there that night. A marine was there who claimed my favorite bed, the only bed with a window. We were not going to argue. The mosquitos might be huge, but all the beds had nets, and he was here first, so who cared?

After a couple of cold beers, I needed to pee. With no bathrooms in the house, I decided to pee out the back door. As I was standing close to the door, I had this terrible feeling that someone was looking at me. I looked to my left—and I was looking straight into the eyes of a Viet Cong!

My heart dropped.

He said in English, "How many GIs here?"

I said, "Maybe five."

He claimed not to be Viet Cong, but I was not sure whether to believe him. He insisted that he worked on the air base for the Americans and had been here before and only wanted to come in for the night and have fun. *What? I thought he was here to kill us.*

I thought maybe he's telling the truth but . . . wait a minute . . .there is a marine upstairs with an M16 rifle.

I cautioned him. "I'll go in first and let everyone know that you will be joining us for the night as a friend."

As I explained to everyone what was going on, I could see the marine looked nervously over at his M16.

I said to him, "Please, don't be stupid. This guy had to sneak off just like you and me to be here, so let's all be friends tonight and enjoy the life we still have."

The marine said, "OK, but I don't want to see him in the morning."

That night was fun but intense. The Vietnamese, who we learned was named Tu, loved to talk with all of the girls. His Vietnamese dialect was hard for me to understand, but I could catch some words. The mama-san brought in a delicious rice dish, although we didn't ask what was in it. I had learned by now not to ask what it was. The marine stayed to himself with one girl and never told us his name.

It was a relief to find when I awoke and looked, both the marine and Tu were gone. It was time to sneak back across the field to meet our Jeep, which would be waiting to pick us up.

A quick goodbye and thank you to the mama-san for keeping us safe . . . As we crossed the field, I could see the Jeep lights crawling along to meet us on the other side. We reached the meeting point, and he slowed down to about five miles per hour, and all four of us jumped on.

Back on the base, we were the talk of the week with the story of the Marine and the Viet Cong. Now, all of my men wanted to go to Bien Hoa village. It also sounded like we had missed a sleepless night in the bunkers as the base was hit again with mortars.

CHAPTER 26

ONE OF THE men known as Speedy Eddy wanted to talk with me in private. As we walked together outside, I flashed back on Eddy when we first met, back when Eddy weighed about 200 pounds. He had probably lost over fifty pounds due to the substance that also gave him the nickname. To my amazement, he wanted me to tell our first sergeant that he was quitting the army. Go ahead and lock him up or do whatever we were going to do. Eddy said he would not be showing up for work, guard duty, roll call, or anything at all. He claimed that his father received a package that he sent, and it meant that he no longer had to work. He didn't tell me what was in that package, but somehow, I didn't think it was legal.

When I finally reported him to our first sergeant, he laughed and said to send him over for a talk. After talking with Eddy, the first sergeant had him arrested. Then he told me that he would try to make sure Eddy got a couple of years in prison for this. Eddy was transferred over to Long Binh Jail (the US Army Installation Stockade, USARVIS, also known as LBJ). I had heard this was a very rough place, and the worst place you could go to in Vietnam!

Some considerable time passed before I heard the end of Eddy's story. He actually only spent a couple of months at Long Binh Jail before he was sent back to the world with a dishonorable discharge. He got off very easy. It was also reported from guys that knew him well that the package that his father received was full of bottles of liquid speed worth over a million dollars.

CHAPTER 27

I WAS FLYING by chopper to Vũng Tàu, a beach town with old hotel resorts built by the French. I was accompanying a couple of warrant officers for the weekend. My duties were to take some orders to deliver, after which I could have two days to myself. I was cautioned, however, that I must not go into the Grand Hotel, as this was off-limits to me.

Wow, a party town right in the middle of a war!

I checked into a dive hotel costing five dollars per night and which was full of GIs. It had no name on the door, so I called it "No-Name Hotel." I took in a couple of bars and met a local girl, "Chinh," who wanted to show me the town. Her English was very good. Around 11:00 p.m., following a great seafood dinner and a few drinks, we ended up at the Grand Hotel. Chinh convinced me to go in as it had the best music in town.

As we walked up to the second floor, I knew that I was in trouble. I looked straight into the eyes of both warrant officers. They had a room there with an open door. On the table in front of them was a large pile of some sort of white blocks. I was taken outside and told to leave and that I did not see anything! I said, "OK, I didn't see anything," and I went on. That must have scared Chinh as she disappeared, and I never saw her again.

The following day, I avoided the officers and did not go near the Grand Hotel. Too bad that I couldn't go in, as it was beautiful. It was a real resort, or at least what I got to see.

The next day, I reported for duty, and I acted as if nothing was wrong. Testing me, one of the officers asked me what I had seen the night before. I said nothing out of the ordinary. The officers then began treating me like I was an old friend. In fact, on the way to Bien Hoa, one told me that they would like me to fly with them more often when delivering orders. Great, I thought, this could give me even more opportunity to travel more through the country. Vietnam has some very beautiful parts to see. It was such a shame that a war was going on here, and everywhere you go, you needed to worry about getting shot.

Back on base, all was fine. The mortars had stopped, at least for a while, as the air force found out where they were coming from and took them out.

All of us in the office had been talking about where to go on R&R (rest and relaxation). The most popular choices were Manila, Taipei, or Hong Kong. Hawaii was the first choice for all of the married men so that they could be with their wives.

Bob and Bill, who both worked in my office, wanted to go to Hong Kong and asked me to go with them. I had the time coming and had no plans, so why not? Yes, I would go with them to Hong Kong.

Having quickly got my paperwork in order, we were off to Hong Kong for a seven-day R&R.

We departed from Saigon at Tan Son Nhut Air Base, and I worried about being shot at from below. But once we got up in the air, it did not take long to get out of Vietnam air space to safety.

Hong Kong was an exciting city. We transferred by taxi to our hotel, which was located on the Kowloon side (mainland). From our room up on the twenty-second floor, you could see over the water to

Hong Kong. What a spectacular view of Hong Kong Harbor. This was *really* living.

The hotel asked us upon checking in if we wanted to meet some local girls, and we met up later that night. Dining, drinks, dancing, yes—Hong Kong has it all for nightlife! The girls, of course, were not free, as this was how they made their living. The escort girls cost us nine dollars each to spend the evening with. We also had to pay for their dinner and, of course, their tea. All three spoke very good English.

In the daytime, we toured Kowloon and Hong Kong. I even had a suit tailor-made for me. It cost eighty dollars. I did not know where I would ever wear it, but it sure looked nice.

That evening, we ended up at the Playboy Club Hong Kong. The girls seemed to know everyone there, including the entertainers. It was not long before we had quite a group sitting around our table, probably because we were buying all of the drinks. When the band found out that I used to play guitar and sing, they invited me up on stage with them to sing a song. Excited, I walked up onto the stage.

My first song went down great, "House of the Rising Sun," and everyone applauded. As I tried to leave the stage, the band yelled, "One more song."

I should have kept walking.

I said, "OK, one more, Play with Fire."

As the band started to play, I knew that I was in trouble. They were playing a song called "Fire," and I did not know it. Oh well, I had enough drinks in me to fake it. I didn't know if anyone really noticed. What a night to remember—getting to sing at the Playboy Club Hong Kong!

Things did not go so well for Bill, as he woke up very sick. As the day went on, the worse he got. Finally, the hotel called for help, and Bill was taken to the hospital. As it turned out, he had food poisoning and had to stay a couple of days in the hospital. Bob and I decided not to go back to Vietnam without him but to wait until he was out of the hospital. This could make us one day late, so I hoped that they did not count us as AWOL . . . but wow, we'd get an extra day in Hong Kong—*yes*.

Our time in Hong Kong was finally over. Bill would get out of the hospital in the morning, in time to make our flight back to Vietnam. He felt cheated on his R&R, as he spent two days in the hospital and thought he was dying.

As we flew back to Vietnam, my mind wandered to thoughts of home and the life I had before the army and how different it was now. I wondered whatever happened to Gerri. Even though I had a few letters from her mother and cousin asking me to write her, I never replied or wrote to Gerri since the "Dear John" letter that I received when I was out in the field, as she made it clear she didn't want me to.

She'd probably met "Jody" back in the world and was getting married by now. I guess I would just wish her the best.

Back on base, all of the guys were waiting to hear our stories of Hong Kong. Everyone laughed about poor Bill ending up in the hospital.

I always tried to get to know all of the men in my platoon. One guy, Joel, was sort of a strange one. He spent every night alone, staring and chanting at candles. One night, I stopped by his hooch and asked what he was doing. He told me that he went home every night. What? I didn't understand, but he claimed that he "sends himself home every night." He said that he could send me home if I would let him. He instructed me to look at the candles, relax, and listen to him, and he would send me home.

I must have dozed off a short time, and when I awoke, Joel claimed that he sent me home. This was weird. I had no memory, but it still was weird.

I could not believe how fast time had been going by. I had almost been in Vietnam for a year, and I was thinking of extending for one more tour (six months). If I did, I would get a thirty-day leave, and get to go home for a month. Wow, home. I could not imagine. It would be so great. Maybe I could try to see my family doctor and find out why I still had stomach cramps almost daily.

After my request for an additional tour was approved, my leave was granted right away, so I sent a letter home, letting everyone know that I would be coming home for a month. I was so excited. I knew Mom would get all of the family together as soon as I got home for a big family dinner.

Chapter 28

I PLANNED TO go up to Reno or Tahoe for a couple of days. I now had a military ID card that stated my age as twenty-one, and I also had one made out for Richard. They looked so genuine that nobody would ever turn these down.

My mama-san, Chi, was not very happy that I was leaving. I had become very close to her, and I had to promise her that I was really coming back.

Chi was originally from North Vietnam. Her late husband and children all fled to the south. Her husband was captured and killed by the NVA. Chi was a loving, sweet lady, but quite old and frail. She was like my "mom" in Vietnam. I loved talking with her, but her stories of life were always so sad.

My flight home was sure a pleasure compared to the one I came over on. This time, I was coming home on a commercial airline, Pan American Airlines, my first real airplane ride that was not a military plane. We departed from Tan Son Nhut Air Base, with a stop in Hawaii and on to Travis Air Base, California. This flight had attendants (stewardesses) serving drinks and meals. Wow, what a difference. With a plane full of GIs returning from Vietnam, the trip was certainly not boring. Everyone seemed to have a different story, and many of them very sad! There was no age requirement on this plane so that all GIs could order drinks.

The excitement was building as we landed at Travis Air Base. I was to take a bus from TAB to Sacramento, where Mom & Dad would pick me up. I felt great, with the exception of a few stomach pains. I couldn't believe that my feet were back in the world.

The bus was full of GIs heading home. Some were being discharged, and others would be going back to Vietnam.

As the bus pulled up to the station, I could see Mom and Dad standing in the crowd. Mom's blond hair and huge smile could be seen fifty feet away. We all just stood there for a moment hugging each other, and Mom had tears pouring down her face.

On the ride home, I heard all about the changes in town and with the family since I had been gone. Tomorrow, we would have a big family dinner get-together so that I could see everyone.

As we drove over the bridge coming into our driveway, I felt very sad that little Gigi, the family poodle, would not be here to greet me. A car hit her last year while she was walking on the road with Dad. The guy never stopped, and Dad said he thought the guy was probably drunk.

Home—I was really home. It felt so good. I wondered why I left in the first place.

Grandma Emily and Aunt Lorean hurried right over to see me. Both of them whispered to me separately to come over and have a beer with them. Neither of my parents drank alcohol, but both Grandma and Aunt Lorean did.

My first night home, I went to bed very early, as I was so exhausted. There were not many things better than getting into your own bed at home. I must have slept for ten hours. It was so good to have no worries of mortars hitting us at night.

THE OTHER SIDE OF NAM

The next day, I felt so good waking up at home. It was wonderful that I still had a full month in front of me.

I called Aunt Nora to check on Cousin Kenny, and he was still OK, but she was very worried about him. He was still out in the field, and it was terrible. He was in combat almost daily. I felt sorry for him.

The next evening was fun to see all of the family. Grandma, aunts, sisters, nieces, nephews, and Richard. Everyone stayed for a big feast of venison that Mom cooked. Our freezer was always full of wild game and fish that my family caught. They were constantly hunting and fishing in the Sierra Nevada Mountain Range.

After dinner, Mom played the piano, and we all joined in singing country and folk songs. It was always so much fun to join in singing around the piano. It brought back happy memories as Mom played the piano almost every night during my childhood.

Mom did have a story for me that was quite shocking. She claimed that a few months ago, she woke up about 6:00 a.m. with me standing at the foot of her bed. She yelled at my dad to "wake up; it's Ike!" As Dad sat up, I disappeared, but I had given her the nicest smile, so she wasn't worried about me because of the way that I smiled at her. Wow, could this have been when that crazy Joel claimed to have sent me home? Did it *really* happen? Unbelievable! When I told Mom the story about Joel sending me back, she was sure of it!

Dad had told me that he would keep my car running while I was away, but he hadn't started it in months, not since he got a speeding ticket and now refuses to drive it. Richard and I worked on the car and finally got it running. Dad claimed the Malibu only had one speed—fast.

It was sure nice to have a car again and be able to drive wherever I wanted to. Richard and I were planning to drive up to Reno in a couple of days now that we both had good fake IDs to make us twenty-one years old.

In the meantime, I started calling some of my old girlfriends to let them know that I was back. I called Cathy first, as she was writing to me in Vietnam. She's the girl my father had met and suggested she write to me. Now she writes to me every week. I had not yet met her, and she was going to college in Chico at the university. She wanted to meet me soon, so we planned a lunch date. I would drive up to Chico, about an hour's drive.

On the drive up there, I started listening to a new 8-track that I just bought. It was so nice to be able to buy music like this. In Vietnam, I only had a small radio with lots of static. These new 8-tracks were like something from the future.

With time to think, I began to reflect on my life. I knew deep down that I should have never joined the army. I should have waited for the draft, and who knows, maybe I would not have been drafted at all. Oh well, no use crying over spilled milk now, and it could be worse. At least I was not out in the field fighting.

Lunch with Cathy was interesting. She was very good looking and becoming quite educated. She was majoring in psychology. She invited me over for a barbeque on Saturday night and said there would be a few other friends stopping by throughout the evening, so I would have an excellent chance to meet some new people.

I also called Joy, who I had taken to the junior prom and dated for a couple of years in high school. We arranged to go to the drive-in to see a movie on Friday night. I couldn't remember the last time I was at a drive-in. It had to have been before I joined the army. I thought how good it would be to see Joy again but reminded myself that she had always seemed to be the marrying kind, and I was not interested in marriage.

Friday evening rolled around quickly, and I meet up with Joy. Her beauty was breath-taking. She got more beautiful every year. The evening was filled with passion. Joy was more romantic than I had ever known her to be. As we were kissing, I kept thinking to myself that I was aware that she was marriage material and not to lead her on. As much as I wanted to go further, I did care for her, and I do not want to be the one to break her heart.

As we kissed at her doorstep, I had a feeling that I would never kiss her again. Perhaps I was a little disappointed, but what should I expect as she had never written to me in Vietnam. I doubted she would remain single long. This was her senior year, and some guy would quickly snap her up.

The next day as I was driving through Live Oak, I happened to notice a friend, Tommy, at the local Foster Freeze. Tommy and I had gone to school together all of our lives, and his mom worked with my mom at King's Market. Mom adored him. She almost regarded him as a son.

He told me he was getting ready to leave for his first tour in Vietnam and was excited about going. He boasted about doing "speed" and said he wanted to try it in Vietnam. Speed? Wow, that stuff could kill you. I was shocked to find that he did drugs. When I graduated from Live Oak, I didn't know anyone who did drugs. He asked me if you could shoot it. I said, "You can't shoot liquid speed! It will kill you. That stuff is pure over there." Tommy just laughed. As I drove off, I worried about him, but I thought to myself he probably would not have to fight in the field since he had been trained as a mechanic. There was a good chance that he could get a rear position.

Saturday evening was my barbecue with Cathy. She lived in a nice apartment complex in Chico, with a pool and Jacuzzi. What a nice way to live.

The barbecue was fun, and about twenty people came by during the evening. Although they were all about my age, they seemed young and naïve compared to my life as a GI in Vietnam. Later that evening, Cathy wanted to talk about what I should do when I got out. She thought that I should enroll full time in college and live at home. I didn't want to make any plans about what to do when I got out. I had to worry about getting out alive first.

I think that she could tell that I was not looking for a relationship but would like our friendship to continue, so we parted with a good night kiss.

The next day, I planned a camping trip with Mom & Dad up by

Grey Eagle. We would fish and maybe take a day trip to Reno since we'd be within an hour's drive.

Camping is always so much fun as Mom does such a good job cooking in the mountains. Everything always tastes so good. We usually had fresh trout and eggs for breakfast, a picnic lunch, and then a wild game dinner such as venison or steak.

Our day trip to Reno was lots of fun. Mom likes to play slots, Dad likes craps, and they both play 21 together. We did not make a killing, but none of us lost very much either.

Dad almost blew it for me with my fake ID when he started talking with a dealer about his own age and said, "and my son here is nineteen." I could not believe it! She had just checked my ID a few moments ago, but she just gave me a strange look and started dealing the cards.

Fishing was good. We ate trout every morning and still had some to bring home.

When we arrived back home, it started to hit me that time was running out, and I would be going back to Nam. With only a couple of weeks left, I decided to call Kathy, a girl I knew, who is from Sutter and a close friend to Gerri. Actually, I had not thought much about Gerri lately, but I was curious to hear what had happened to her, thinking she was probably married or with Jody by now.

Kathy answered the phone when I called and was very excited to hear from me. She was now engaged to be married in a couple of months but agreed to meet with me for old time's sake.

I asked her about Gerri.

"Oh my God, Ike, you don't know?"

"Know what?"

Kathy said, "Let's go now and drive down to Sacramento for dinner. I'll tell you on the way."

As we drove to Sacramento, she started to tell me the story. She asked me if I remembered the first time I met Gerri. We were at a party, we'd gone into a bedroom, and then she sort of passed out on me.

"Yes, I came to get you, and you sat with her until she came back around in a little while."

Kathy explained this hadn't been the only time this had happened, and that Gerri used to pass out in school occasionally and turn blue.

She told me sadly, "Ike, Gerri died last year from leukemia. She died at only eighty-six pounds with no hair and looked so bad that she did not want you to see her. *That* is why she wrote you that 'Dear John' letter. She knew she was dying."

I was shocked. None of her family or friends ever told me. The few letters that I received from her mom and cousin never explained why I shouldn't write back. I felt sick. Tears rolled down my face. Kathy had me stop at the cemetery in Lincoln, and we walked out to Gerri's grave. It was a very difficult, emotional experience.

We later went to dinner, but it was not so great as it was such a sad evening. But it was good to see Kathy and learn about her new love.

The next morning was also sad as I told Mom and Dad what had happened to Gerri. They never even had the opportunity of meeting her but felt bad for me. I decided to drive down to Lincoln, where Gerri lived to see if her mom was still there.

So that afternoon, as I drove down their long driveway alongside a peach orchard, I could see some of the family walking out on the porch to see who was coming. As I stopped the car, I heard a voice say, "Look Mom, it's Ike. I told you that he would come back."

It was such a beautiful and sad reunion. When we walked into the living room, I noticed the picture of Gerri and me together. I explained that I did not know about her illness, and they said that Gerri hadn't wanted me to, as she wanted me to remember her as she was.

The family was getting ready to move back to Oklahoma, as they could not afford to live in California any longer. I had been lucky to catch them since they would be moving in the next couple of weeks. It was a very nice visit, and I feel honored to know such a loving family.

Driving home that night, I started thinking about how much my life had changed since leaving high school. I was now nineteen years old, but I felt much older. Vietnam was always on my mind. I knew it would not be long before I would be going back. I just heard on the news about another firefight . . . twelve Viet Cong dead, no American casualties. It reminded me of when I was out in the field with the 101st Airborne. I could visualize the guys running about a mile from where the fighting was and then call in napalm, or, worse yet, they stood and fought with limited firepower, numbering only about eleven men. I felt sorry for all of the men still in combat. When would this war end, and why were they still fighting?

CHAPTER 29

THE NEXT DAY, I drove over to Richard's house. He had followed his dream and became a real farmer. He was leasing land from other owners and sharing the profits. Richard drove me around, showing me the prune orchards and walnut orchards that he tended. He did a lot of the work himself but did have a few employees working for him. He was so proud and loved to show me around his orchards.

Dinner was always a fun time at home, and you never knew who might drop by. Mom started cooking as soon as she got home from work unless Dad started sooner. We all liked to cook.

As the weekend approached, my folks decided to go to Reno with me. Richard could not go this time, as he was busy irrigating a new orchard that he just acquired.

We decided to camp outside Grey Eagle and drive over to Reno for the day. That way, we could fish the stream near our campsite and maybe have fresh trout and eggs for breakfast.

After setting up camp, the three of us set out trout fishing. It was a nice time of day, early evening, and the fish were just starting to bite.

All three of us caught trout, but Mom caught the largest at thirteen inches.

That evening, we sat around the campfire and listened to Dad reminisce about the old days when he was a young boy, and he and his dad used to hunt and fish together. I could tell that he was wishing that I still lived at home so I could go hunting and fishing with him.

Breakfast was excellent . . . trout and eggs. It just did not get much better in camping. After breakfast, we drove over to Reno for the day.

This time, I was quite surprised to see how many guys were in uniform . . . lots of young, military guys. We had a great time. Dad won $400 on craps and gave me $100. I was almost $100 down, but I still felt like a winner. My military ID worked fine, and it was a good thing as I noticed the new California driver's license would no longer be easy to change. The picture was not the same if you were under twenty-one. I don't think I could even change the new ones.

It was dark when we arrived back at camp. We quickly built a fire, and Mom started making dinner. That night, I told my parents more about Vietnam and the people. I had made many friends in Vietnam, both American and Vietnamese. The Vietnamese people were very proud, and many believed they were defending their country against a United States attempt to invade. Not surprisingly, not one Vietnamese had ever tried to invade the United States. It did make me wonder what we were doing over there.

July 20, 1969, Apollo 11 landed on the moon!

Man on the moon. How exciting! This could change the world. Mom thought that I should see my grandpa Joe in the nursing home as he had asked about me. Grandpa Joe just turned 101 and had been saying for years that he would not die until he saw a man on the moon.

As Grandpa Joe saw me walking into the nursing home, he said, "They did it. They put a man on the moon." He was so excited to see me and tell me this. Grandpa Joe was very frail but could still walk with a walker. He was originally from Maui, Hawaii, and at age fourteen, he jumped on a Chinese ship in the bay as a stowaway. He spent eight years in China and jumped another ship to Europe. He was eighty-six years old when he met my grandma Emily and was never married before. She was the one and only. Grandpa Joe could read and write in seven different languages.

My last night at home was wonderful. About twenty family members and friends were at my going-away dinner. We had elk steaks for dinner, one of my favorites. I promised Dad that when I came home again in six months, I would go deer hunting with him for a week, as it would be the opening of the season. He really liked that idea and would start planning now on where to go.

It was very sad saying goodbye, but it was time. Mom had tears pouring down her face, and I thought Dad might have also been crying. As the bus left the depot, I looked back at my parents, and tears were streaming down my face.

I quickly pulled out of it as I was sitting in a bus full of GIs leaving for Vietnam. I was not going straight back, however, but meeting up with two guys from my unit, Chuck and Monte, and we were going to party for a couple of days in San Francisco.

The bus trip was only two hours, and I was in San Francisco. I called the hotel from the depot and found out that Chuck and Monte had already arrived. A quick cab ride and I arrived at the hotel where the guys were waiting for me. We all wanted to talk at the same time as we had stories—so many stories—about our leave to tell. We had an evening full of stories and laughs. It was so funny to see Monte flirt with every girl as he was from New Jersey, and he wanted a California girl so badly.

Of course, being GIs and not knowing the city at all, we wound up in the worst of places. Monte kept asking for girls, and everywhere we went just got worse. One guy told him that if he wanted a beautiful California girl that he could get him one, but it would cost him fifty dollars. Monte wanted to do it, but he wanted Chuck and me to go with him for security. Chuck and I laughed, as there was no way that we were going to pay fifty dollars for a girl, but we agreed to go with him for back up.

After walking for maybe ten blocks, Monte's new friend said that the girls were here. He would need to go in first and then come back out for Monte. In just one minute, the guy came back out and said to Monte that he had his choice of two California girls, a blonde or brunette. Monte wanted the blonde and gave the guy fifty dollars. The guy said to wait here again and went in to pay the girl, and then he would call for Monte.

After about ten minutes, we all felt something was wrong. Monte went up the stairs and knocked on the door, but nobody answered. I yelled, "Try the door and see if it's open."

He opened the door . . . only to find it went down a flight of stairs and back outside. Both Chuck and I broke out in big laughs. Monte had just been taken in San Francisco! Wait until we told all of the guys back in Nam. The harder we laughed, the angrier Monte got. Finally, he started yelling for a police officer.

The next thing I knew, here was a cop, and he was not very happy with Monte. Monte was demanding that they needed to find this thief who stole his money. The policeman informed Monte he could be arrested for trying to buy a prostitute. When Monte realized this, his attitude changed. Another policeman walked up and said, "Let him go. They're on their way to Vietnam." He asked when we flew out, and I told him tomorrow. He said to go back to our hotel and stay there, almost like it was an order.

We spent the rest of the night back at the hotel bar, where it was a little safer. Chuck and I could not help but laugh all night at Monte. He pleaded with us not to tell anyone else about the incident, and right away, Chuck told some GIs he just met at the bar. The whole bar broke out into laughter. Even Monte finally joined in when he learned of other guys that got ripped off the same way. Oh well, so much for the California girl.

The next day, it was off to Vietnam. The plane was full of GIs traveling back. The mood was very somber; there was no more laughter. We flew over Hawaii, where we refuelled. It was so beautiful flying over the islands. I promised myself that someday, I would come to Hawaii for a visit, but first, I needed to live through Nam again.

CHAPTER 30

WELCOME BACK TO Vietnam . . .

Coming back was very difficult after a month at home in California. Wow, what a shock! It was hard to believe that this was real.

There had been a lot of Viet Cong activity at night, and everyone was on edge. The sirens were going off several times, calling us to the bunkers.

Incoming mortars, here they come!

The boom was tremendous as they hit.

I seemed more afraid now than before I went on leave.

As I relaxed in bed, my mind started drifting. I thought of basic training with Kenny. I laughed to myself when I remembered the time that I looked over at him, and he was standing in formation . . . asleep. Sergeant White was not pleased and was screaming as loud as he could, "Denney, how can you stand up straight and sleep? *Nobody* can do that!"

But Kenny could.

As daylight approached, the mortars stopped, and we were up to start the day.

This was my first day back, so it was fun to see everyone, even under these circumstances. That evening, a Vietnamese band was playing at the NCO bar, performing some of the most popular American songs of the time. Some of the guys were talking of plans to go to Saigon for the weekend or sneaking into Bien Hoa village for a night. I knew that I would get back in the swing of things, but at the moment, it seemed like going off base was getting a little risky just to have a little fun.

I was only back two weeks when I received a letter from Mom telling me that my friend Tommy had died in Vietnam. He had just arrived and apparently "shot liquid speed" his very first week. I was shocked! It felt so bad to think I had just recently seen him and knew what he was going to do—and he *really* did it. He would not listen to me. Sometimes, when a person has their mind made up, words will not change their mind. I decided to go to the NCO bar for a cold beer and have a toast to Tommy.

The sirens ended my night at the NCO bar as we all headed for our bunkers. This time, they only sounded off for about an hour as the air force located and destroyed the mortar positions. As I settled in for the night, I wondered about Kenny. Where was he? Was he okay?

CHAPTER 31

TIME GOES BY fast when you are having fun, or so they say. I had already been back in Vietnam for a month, and yet, it seemed like yesterday that I was home.

Major Sherburn, our new Major, wrote a letter to all of our loved ones back home so they would know how important our mission was:

DEPARTMENT OF THE ARMY
Headquarters, US Army Support Command, Saigon
Personnel Services Center
APO 96491

AVCA SGN PS   1 October 1969

To the Folks at Home: Travis family

This letter is the first in a series that I will periodically write to provide you with news concerning your son in the 520th/537th Personnel Services Center. First, I would like to introduce myself.

I am Major John H. Sherburn, and I have been the Chief of the Personnel Services Center since August 1969. Our unit's mission is to provide personnel administrative support to units assigned or attached to the United States Support Command, Saigon. Administrative support is personnel administration involving the custody and maintenance of individuals' personnel records; the processing of personnel actions; and providing services for the primary benefit of individuals, e.g., request for leave, request for discharge, transportation arrangements, etc., and those for commanders, e.g., personnel data and reports to permit them to effectively discharge their personnel management duties. Additionally, we are charged with the responsibility for collecting and grouping personnel information to provide ready analysis for decisions; responding to requirements of higher headquarters; operating the Command's replacement system; and furnishing decisions on personnel actions and exercising staff supervision of personnel administrative activities in subordinate units. Our mission requires us to maintain approximately 20,000 personnel records for 269 units located throughout III and IV Corps areas of the Republic of Vietnam.

To perform its mission, the Personnel Services Center is organized along functional lines. The Center Headquarters consists of myself, an administration officer, the sergeant major, and warrant officers. We have six composite teams that are under the direct control of the Chief of the Personnel Division. Each team consists of a warrant officer, personnel sergeant and twenty-one enlisted personnel. Each team maintains approximately 2,500 records and provides complete personnel services to the unit supported.

Although our principal mission is to provide personnel administrative support, we are also charged with the defence of a portion of the Bien Hoa Army Base-Air Force Base complex. Because of the critical importance of tactical aircraft, the facilities here at Bien Hoa are subjected to periodic enemy rocket and mortar attacks. Sergeant Travis has been instrumental in thwarting all ground attacks directed at this installation, and his actions in the face of the enemy has brought praise and commendation! I consider it a distinct honor and privilege to command men who have proved their diligence and bravery!

Our regular hail and farewell party was held on 23 September. This is a monthly affair to welcome all new arrivals and to say farewell to all repartees. These parties serve more or less as a get-acquainted session for old-timers with the new arrivals. I might add there is an outstanding comradeship among the members of the Center.

Please remember how important receiving mail from home is. That one contact with home, a daily letter, though it is a relatively small endeavor, is often all that is required to maintain the spirit and morale of your loved one here in the Personnel Services Center.

Religious activities are also an integral part of the life within the Personnel Services Center. In addition to regular Christian Worship Services conducted on post, personnel are permitted to attend other religious services conducted on Long Binh post and downtown Saigon. Of course, attendance at religious services in Saigon is based on the level of combat activity in the vicinity.

In the event of an emergency at home, remember to contact the Red Cross. Your local chapter has the most direct means of communication in Vietnam.

If you have any question or problem, please feel free to write me.

Sincerely,
John H. Sherburn
Major, AGC Chief

CHAPTER 32

I HEARD FROM Mom that Kenny was still okay. She had been talking with his mom, my aunt Nora. It seems he was having a very hard time in Vietnam as he was with the 82nd Airborne working in the Mekong Delta. He was an infantry grenadier like I was, carrying the M79 grenade launcher. I thought of him soaking wet in a rice paddy in the monsoons every time it rained.

I had been to the company medics again for my stomach pains. They were getting worse as I had the cramps more often. The medic told me that it must be in my head, and he wanted me to talk to a shrink. I didn't know . . . maybe I was starting to lose it?

I received another letter from Mom telling me that Kenny was taken to the hospital for a week of observation after his best friend was killed in front of him. She didn't know the details, except that Kenny was with him when he died. Kenny's parents were very upset and concerned about him because he was in shock.

When I heard this, I decided it was time to have Kenny pulled from the field and brought to me. I hatched a plan to get him one week with "Top Secret Orders." If I could pull this off, I would take Kenny to Saigon for a little vacation and rest. A little in-country R&R, good food, and fun is what he needed. Life was what you made it, even in Vietnam, and Kenny needed a break!

I rose early in the morning and began making plans to have Kenny sent to me with "top secret orders." All of the guys in my office were behind me, and even egging me on. Hopefully, I could pull this off if I could convince everyone to believe me. I started with a call (walkie-talkie) from my office to Command Headquarters, requesting to be transferred to the 82nd Airborne. I found out that I had to go through Saigon USARV Headquarters to transfer the phone call to the 82nd Airborne. I also learned it would take General Abrams, the general of US Forces in Vietnam, to authorize orders to bring Kenny to me on a top-secret order. I called back and made the order in the name of General Abrams!

I informed the operator that he must put me through to the 82nd Airborne, or he would be a Private E2 by nightfall. After about an hour of being bounced around from one operator to another and having to threaten all of them with being demoted, I was finally transferred to Kenny's unit. I explained to the radio operator that I need Kenneth Denney to be flown to Tan Son Nhut Air Base immediately for a one-week "top-secret mission." His orders would be given to his superior upon arrival at the airport.

At this point, I had yet to figure out how to do this without actually forging General Abrams's signature?

The radioman put his sergeant on the walkie-talkie, and I explained to him what I wanted and expected. He wanted to know who I was and on whose authority I was giving this order. I told him I was Sgt. Travis, and this came directly from General Abrams. He then put Kenny on the phone, and I could tell that he was shocked to hear my voice!

"Kenny, I am bringing you to party with me for one week on top-secret orders. Do you understand? Over."

"Yes, sir, over."

"Do they really believe me? Over."

"Yes, sir, over."

"Give me back to your sergeant so that I can make arrangements to pick you up at Tan Son Nhut Air Base in Saigon, over."

His sergeant did believe me and had Kenny board the helicopter immediately to fly him out. I called my friend Jim in the motor pool for a Jeep to pick Kenny up when he arrived, and I told him all about the plan as we drove to Saigon to meet Kenny. I hoped the plan would work. Would he really be there? If not, I was in *big* trouble. I started to feel a little sick at what the consequences might be if I were caught. Was it worth it? I thought so.

As we pulled up to the gate at Tan Son Nhut Air Base, I handed the guard a copy of an order I made up. He looked it over and flagged me on without hesitation.

Tan Son Nhut Air Base was a very active base with airplanes and helicopters coming in only seconds apart. We drove over to the area where we could see the choppers landing, and there he was . . . Ken Denney waiting for me as if this were a taxi stand!

Everything seemed to be going well, but with all of the military personnel standing around, I knew I had to look the part, so I was very stern when we pulled up to him, and I announced, "Corporal Kenneth Denney, I am here to escort you to Bien Hoa Army Base." Actually, we both wanted to jump up and down, but we had to be cool.

Then, a warrant officer yelled, "Sergeant, I want those orders." He marched over to me again and demanded, "I want those orders, and now!"

I instructed Corporal Denney to get in the back of the Jeep; then I handed the warrant officer a manila envelope that read: *"Top Secret."* I quickly jumped into the front seat of the Jeep as the officer examined the envelope and yelled, "It's empty!"

I yelled back, "Of course, this is a top-secret mission! You will get a copy in one week when I return Corporal Denney. Be here at the same time in one week, and you will get your orders."

I saluted him and told my driver to go. As we drove out of the base, I breathed a sigh of relief. "We did it," and we both started screaming and laughing.

"Do you believe we really pulled this off?"

Kenny said, "I never thought of anything like this, but when I heard your voice on the radio, I knew that you could pull this off."

We had a great time driving back to Bien Hoa, laughing and talking. Kenny mentioned how he would like to be able to come back to Saigon during the week and take in a few bars. I laughed and told him, "Don't worry, you will. I'm going to show you Vietnam, as you have never known it. I'm going to show you "the *other* side of Nam."

As we pulled up to my hooch in Bien Hoa Army Base, Chi (my mama-san) was waiting for us with a big smile. Chi did not smile very much, but when I had told her what I was doing, she got a kick out of it. Chi looked at Kenny and said, "Oh no, your body is bad." He did look dirty, like he has been living in the same clothes for a month and sleeping in the swamps. As it turned out, he was. She had to cut the pants off of him as they were actually stuck to his legs. He had sores, bug bites, and ringworm all over his body, so Chi had him take a shower, and then she treated his sores. Chi said his legs looked so bad she wasn't sure if she could heal him in only one week!

Kenny had been working in the Delta, a very wet area of Vietnam. He was in the infantry, sleeping on the ground every day. His stories were chilling, as he talked about the frequent firefights and sometimes the close in-fighting. Always wet and cold, or hot or both. His living conditions were miserable, and his body was showing it. Although he was still only nineteen, he looked closer to forty. The war was really taking its toll on his body.

He cleaned up pretty good and said he sure felt better with a little medication and clean, dry clothes. Kenny was about the same size as me, so he fit into my clothes, which was a good thing because he was traveling like he lived in the field . . . with nothing.

After dinner at the mess hall, I took Kenny into the NCO Club to hear some music, a live Vietnamese band. This was one of the few times that he had heard live music since he left the world. He met several of my friends that I worked with and heard stories about Saigon and sneaking into Bien Hoa village for the night. He could not believe how I was living in Vietnam compared to him, but he was delighted to be here. We shared stories, tears, and laughter for most of the night. Thankfully, it was also a very peaceful night as the sirens only went off once.

In contrast, Kenny's stories were very hard to listen to. His world was a world of snipers, wet, cold firefights, and killing almost daily!

He talked about his friend, Don, dying in front of him. Don was walking in front of Kenny when he tripped a wire. He put his hands in the air and turned to look Kenny in the eyes. They were only about ten feet away from each other. For nearly two seconds, it was as if his friend were saying goodbye. Then there was an explosion, and Kenny landed about another ten feet away covered in blood. He thought that he was dying. Then he realized that the blood and body parts were not his, but his friend, Don. Kenny went into shock, and they had to medevac him out for a seven-day observation. After seven days in a field hospital, they sent him back into combat.

He told me about the worst firefight that he was involved in, working in an area called the Hobo Woods. One guy, in particular, stood out in these stories. They called him Bone. He was an American Indian. Bone would practice throwing his knife whenever he could, constantly, every day, and Kenny thought that he was a little annoying.

One day while walking in the woods, the unit was attacked. Viet Cong (VC) had set up a trap to surround the men. As the fight continued, the ammunition ran low. There was no air support as the radioman was hit and had made no contact with Command Headquarters. Their sergeant realized this and ran to the radioman on the ground, grabbed the radio, and called Command. As he did so, he heard a noise in the brush—a Viet Cong. He took his M16 rifle, only to find an empty chamber. The Viet Cong stepped out of the brush, pointing an

AK-47 at him. He knew it was over! Suddenly, without any sound, the Viet Cong went flying backward with a huge knife stuck in his chest. Bone threw the knife from at least twenty feet away. Soon after this, help arrived.

Kenny also mentioned he sent a letter to his mom asking her to send him a 9-mm automatic. Being a grenadier, he carried the M79, but he still wanted a fast sidearm for protection. I agreed, because when I was with the 101st carrying the M79, I had no sidearm, and it would make a huge difference in close combat.

Another story Kenny recalled was about the fighting at the Fucung Bridge. He was in such close combat that he had to fire the M79 using Beehive rounds. These are like huge shotgun shells made for close-up shooting. I did not have these rounds with the 101st, but Kenny was issued them—a good thing!

He also told me the story of his chemical warfare school. I had to roll in laughter after hearing how horrible it was. He said that they were literally gassed every day with some type of chemical gas. It started his very first day there in the outhouse. The door would not open, and gas was pouring in. Welcome to chemical warfare school. I was so pleased to have missed that one.

The morning after his arrival, Kenny got to meet the guys that I work with in the office, and they all wished us a fun and safe time for the week. They would cover my work most of the days so that I could spend time with Kenny. My friends at the motor pool already had it set up so that I could get a Jeep or some type of transportation throughout the week. Kenny could not believe all of the favors that I was getting.

I told him, "Oh, don't worry. They will all be calling in the favors that I owe in the near future. On this base, we all take care of each other."

Kenny had a hard time eating breakfast, as he was not used to eating so much. No doubt, he would gain a few pounds in the next week, and he certainly needed it. I told him that for the first couple of days that we would lie low, giving him time to rest up and heal, and then midweek, we would venture into Saigon for a couple of days. Also, this would give me time at my office to make sure that some work was getting done during the week. I knew that if I was not there, my guys did not work very much—or at all.

That night after another meal at the mess hall, we went back over to the NCO Club to listen to some music and plan our week.

During the evening, we heard the horrific news of the My Lai Massacre. Everyone on the base was talking about it. An entire village of old people, women, and children—raped and slaughtered by US Forces! It was horrendous and had been covered up since March of 68. Both Kenny and I wondered what horrible training centers these monsters went through before arriving in Vietnam. Sounded like some of these men went through Camp Crockett!

Chapter 33

On a chosen day, we left early in the morning for Saigon so that we would have the entire day to get there. We had a Jeep, an armed driver, and orders cut, allowing us to travel to Saigon and stop at Long Binh Army Base, if needed.

The drive itself from Bien Hoa to Saigon was quite an experience, never knowing what we might encounter on the way, and Kenny just couldn't believe that I travelled around Vietnam like this without being killed.

I said, "Kenny, every day, you could be killed in Vietnam." You might as well enjoy it while you're alive. If you can see past the war, Vietnam is a beautiful country, and the people are as loving as any could be. I have many Vietnamese friends, and I trust them with my life! Chi, my mama-san at my hooch, is like family, like a mom. Co Huong, my friend here on the base, is a sweet as she can be. I also have Vietnamese friends that I feel completely safe with in Saigon and Bien Hoa village.

Kenny responded that every time he saw a Vietnamese out in the field, they started shooting. His life and experiences were totally different in active combat to mine on a rear base.

No clouds in the sky today. It was a little humid, but that was okay. Kenny was really starting to enjoy himself. He was beginning to dry out from the rain and heal up. Within a few minutes of leaving Bien Hoa Army Base, I pointed out the large field that we cross late at night on foot when we sneak into Bien Hoa village. It was a very dangerous field as both sides would shoot anyone seen crossing, and there were helicopter/gunships with lights sweeping the field armed with .50-caliber machine guns. If they saw any movement at all, they would shoot to kill.

Kenny said, "Wow, I don't know if I really want to do that or not."

I thought to myself *good*, as I did not want to take any real chances like that with him. I would never be able to face Aunt Nora if anything happened to Kenny when he was with me!

Thirty minutes later, I pointed out that if we turned left, we would go to Long Binh Army Base. I told Kenny it was not a place I liked because it held horrible memories of when I first arrived in the country. I would never forget the first smell of Long Binh Army Base.

Kenny started laughing and said, "You stirred shit too?"

We both broke out laughing, as it turned out Kenny also arrived in Vietnam through Long Binh Army Base. He had the same experience that I did. He had spent nine days "stirring shit" all day, smelling it, and being covered in the smoke for the entire time. Yikes, no wonder he said he was so relieved to go out into the field finally.

The rest of our ride to Saigon went pretty quick, and the excitement was building up as we approached the city. As I've said before, Saigon was huge. People were everywhere, going all directions at the same time. Kenny took pictures most of the way. He loved to take pictures.

I told our driver to drop us off on Tran Hung Dau Street at the Milan Hotel. Kenny should get a kick out of this place, as it was wild! Tran Hung Dau Street was very busy, as usual. GIs were everywhere as the street was lined with bars and girls at every doorway. I thought Kenny surely must have been running out of film by now.

As we pulled up in front of the Milan Hotel, I pulled out my bag of cigarettes. Kenny said, "What's that for?" I explained to him that these eight cartons of cigarettes were going to pay for the next two nights here for rooms, food, drinks—everything.

Kenny said, "I still can't believe the way you live in Vietnam . . . Unbelievable."

"Just believe it and enjoy it."

We first walked into the bar for a beer. It was always fun to be recognized, and, yes, here came several girls and the mama-san who recognized me. I explained that we didn't want girls; we just wanted to have a few beers and talk.

Mama-san came up to me and said, "Chicken Man," her name for me, "do you have something for me?"

"Yes," I replied as I handed her my bag of cigarettes.

"How long do you stay?"

"Two nights."

"Two nights? Okay."

I warned Kenny to be careful of the girls that you talk with, as you might end up buying them tea and would not even know it, but he already knew that much at least.

A Saigon Tea Girl hustled tea at the bar from the GIs in exchange for their company. The tea glass is tiny so that she could always ask you to buy her another tea. That way, they were earning money by getting the GIs to spend more.

That night, the place was packed with GIs. Obviously, we were not the only two that got away from our units. There were so many beers being ordered at the same time that it took a while to get a drink.

The girls were driving us crazy as they all were trying to speak some English. They went by numbers, not by names, so it was easy for the guys to remember the ones they liked. Several of the girls told us we look like number one. Number one was good. Number ten was bad.

Because I like to practice my Vietnamese with them, I got to know some by name. Tee and Son were sort of "friends" of mine, as I knew them from being here before. Both girls tried talking with Kenny, but they hardly spoke any English, and Kenny spoke no Vietnamese. Some of the girls spoke pretty good English, so Kenny did have some fun talking with them and buying tea.

I always buy a lot of tea. A tea cost about forty cents US. The girls that I knew explained to me that without the tea money, they could not feed their family or children. In Vietnam, there was no welfare program, no unemployment, or disability. They must do whatever it took to make money for food. How sad. You learned to respect these girls quickly when you realize that with the tea money, they were feeding the entire family . . . sometimes, the parents, grandparents, aunts, uncles, and children. Their stories reminded me of the stories my dad used to tell me about his Depression days as a young boy living on an Indian Reservation.

I could tell that Kenny really liked this bar. He was ordering more beers and got in a long conversation with some other GI about being out in the field.

I asked mama-san to get us some rice with beef. The smell was strange for Kenny, and he would not eat it. Although there were no other choices for dinner, Kenny said he couldn't eat, as it did not look like beef. He was sure that it was dog. It may have been, but I thought it was okay, and I had eaten it before.

The next day was quite an adventure, especially for Kenny. We decided to have a driver show us around, or at least to the safe areas that I knew of. This was good for Kenny taking pictures. When you saw some parts of Saigon, you realized that it was also a beautiful city. It could almost make you forget that there was a war going on.

Our cab was not like any cab back in the world. It was a motorcycle with a seat on the front (rickshaw) for us to sit on—and hang on to for dear life. The driver zipped in and out of traffic and had several near collisions—what an experience. Our hangovers did not help us either.

That evening, Kenny wanted a good steak. I took him to the President Hotel, where I thought the restaurant there had some of the best beef in Vietnam. It should be as it was from Australia. Kenny loved it. He said it was the best dinner that he had had since leaving home.

That night, we partied a bit at the President Hotel. It was sort of like the Milan Hotel but a little more upper class. Most of the Tea Girls could speak good English, so it made it much easier for Kenny.

After two nights in Saigon, we were on our way back to Bien Hoa Army Base. Kenny only had a few more nights; then he would have to go back out to the field.

Jimmy from the motor pool had picked us up at 4:00 p.m., as planned. The ride back was about one and a half hours and was a little scary as he explained how the road was getting hit with snipers, or vehicles were being ambushed. Jimmy had an M16 in the Jeep, and Kenny held it all of the way back to Bien Hoa Army Base, ready to shoot. Luckily, we made it back safely.

CHAPTER 34

TONIGHT, WE WERE just going to kick back and do nothing, not even go to the NCO Club. At the chow hall, we laughed with some of the guys over stories of Saigon, and then Kenny heard a few from Bien Hoa village.

Now, he wanted to go to Bien Hoa village. He had heard enough about it and knew that I have been there and begged me to take him. I told him I would think about it over a good night's sleep.

Bien Hoa village, the entrance to Bien Hoa city, was off-limits. It is Viet Cong-controlled, and many GIs died there in the Tet of '68.

I had promised myself that I wouldn't risk taking Kenny there, but now, I was thinking of taking him.

Kenny had one older sister, Pat, who, like my sister, Arvella, watched over us as children like a second mother. Pat would be upset with me if she ever found out that I would risk taking Kenny to such a dangerous place.

Several explosions could be heard throughout the night, but none close enough to the base to sound the alarms. Good, because I did not want to spend the night in the bunkers.

The following morning, Kenny still wanted me to take him to Bien Hoa village. He wanted me to take him that night so that he would still have a couple of days to just hang around the base to rest up before he went back.

"OK, if we are going to go, let's go tonight."

Chi, my mama-san, heard us talking about going into Bien Hoa village and said that I "butterfly" too much. She thought we should stay on the base and just go to the NCO Club. I told her we would do that too but decided we would go to Bien Hoa village after the NCO Club.

That night, after a few beers at the NCO Club, it was getting late enough to make our trip. I had a driver arranged already for drop-off and morning pickup. I had orders made up to leave the base.

I always got a little nervous when I handed the guard at the gate our orders to leave the base, but there was no problem. He just looked at the orders and handed them back, saying, "Have fun, Ike," as he opened the gate.

The Jeep slowed down to a crawl, and both Kenny and I jumped off and rolled in the field. There were no choppers or planes in the air, so we both started running across the field. When the chopper lights did appear, we hit the ground and lay there until they crossed over. Then we jumped up and ran the rest of the way across the field as fast as we could.

It was very dark out as clouds were covering the sky, and visibility was poor. I had told Kenny that we would run into the girls on the other side of the field and then follow them to a safe house.

All of a sudden, I heard a scream and thump. I saw that Kenny and some girl were both on the ground. He had run right into her.

I bent over to help them up. Luckily, they both got up unharmed, and we followed the girl into the safe house. Kenny was very nervous about being in Bien Hoa village and said that he had money to pay for security, if that was possible. Mama-san recognized me from before and knew that I wanted food, beer, and smoke.

She asked, "How much will you give me if I give you all the girls, nine of them? We will let nobody else in. I will bring you plenty of beer, food, smoke, and have the girls stand at both doors for security for the night."

Kenny agreed and said, "I have US$200 on me, and I will give it all to you for this one night if I get out of here alive." He was terrified. Looking out the window at Viet Cong walking the streets carrying AK-47s. I told him to stay away from the window and not to look out.

Mama-san quickly took the money, and I told Kenny that he paid way too much. He said, "I don't care. I just want a fun night and live through it." Kenney was actually shaking!

The girls were "fun." They always are in Bien Hoa village. They get very few American GIs that sneak in as we did. Kenny did have a hard time talking with them as only a couple could speak any English at all, unlike the girls in Saigon. I had no trouble as my Vietnamese had become fairly good.

We enjoyed cold beer, good smoke, and a food selection that I thought to be the best I have seen in Bien Hoa village. We had shrimp, rice, and something that I could not recognize. Kenny did eat some shrimp and rice and thought it was pretty good.

Girls surrounded Kenny. I told mama-san in Vietnamese, "Just have them sit close to him, act like they are interested, and he will drink beer and tell stories until he passes out." After he'd had a few beers, he calmed down and began having the time of his life. We laughed and told stories most of the night. The girls laughed too, even though I was aware that they did not have a clue what we were saying.

Very early the next morning, mama-san woke us up before daylight, as promised. We said our goodbyes and thanked her. The girls quickly walked us to the field.

We were off and running across the field, although Kenny was complaining he had a hangover from too much beer. Luckily, no gunships in the air this morning, so we should be able to cross the field quickly. I could see our Jeep in the distance, but Kenny had to stop and vomit. I urged him on. It was almost daylight, and we couldn't be seen out here. Finally, after two stops, we made it to the Jeep.

What a relief.

Our driver told us that the base had been hit all night, and they spent most of the night inside the bunkers. In fact, he said that he heard the major was looking for me to work as sergeant of the guard last night as he said I was needed on the berm. Oh well, I would give him some excuse.

Back on base, things were quiet as most of the men were trying to get some sleep in the daytime from being up on guard in the bunkers all night. Kenny and I were both ready for some rest too, so we joined in on the daytime sleep.

That night we were up, rested, and having big laughs and telling stories from the Bien Hoa village experience. Kenny said that Bien Hoa village was the most fun and exciting place that he had ever been in his entire life! I think the danger had a lot to do with it.

The next day was very sad, as it is the day that I had to take Kenny back to Tan Son Nhut Air Base to go back to his unit. He was very quiet on the ride back. I could not imagine what he must be thinking as he was going back out to the field to fight.

As we approached the chopper waiting for him, I could see a warrant officer, the pilot, standing outside of it. We saluted him, and he asked to see the orders. Just like the previous occasion, I handed him a large envelope that read "Top Secret." He opened it and looked at me, shocked.

"This is empty," he yelled. "Where are the orders?"

I replied assertively, "The orders are top secret, and my orders are not to discuss it with anyone. If there's a problem, I have been instructed to get the name, rank, and service number of the person who is questioning me, and he will be a private by nightfall. I just need to get your full name and service number, and you will be notified of your future status."

He stared at me, alarmed for a moment, and then agreed.

"It's okay."

He would fly Kenny back to his unit. I saluted him and nodded at Kenny as we left. On the drive back to Bien Hoa Army Base, I could not keep my mind off of Kenny and what he may face in the field. I hoped and prayed that he made it through the rest of his tour.

Some considerable time later, I found out from Kenny that the warrant officer had confided in him that he had worked out what was going on. He believed Kenny was a direct relative of General Abrams, the U.S. general of Vietnam, and that he really never went on a top-secret mission but actually spent a week in Saigon with General Abrams. Wow, was he ever wrong!

For the rest of his tour, everyone thought that Kenny was really a family member of General Abrams.

CHAPTER 35

AFTER CATCHING UP on my work, I went to see our medic. Again, I came out with no answers about why I had stomach cramps, which were now becoming daily.

I quickly threw myself into catching up with my work while enjoying the fact that I was the talk of the base. Everyone was talking about what I did getting Kenny out of the field. However, I was getting a little worried the wrong officers might hear about it and do something.

Not everyone here enjoyed hearing the stories. Several officers warned me about getting "carried away." Also, I got a few frowns from some of the older men. But some guys kept asking me to take them with me the next time I planned a trip into Bien Hoa village.

Co Huong was not impressed either. She worked in the mess hall and lived in Bien Hoa City. She was very cute but did have a local Vietnamese boyfriend on the base. He also worked in the mess hall. Co Huong was so afraid that I would be killed going into Bien Hoa village. She would always say, "Chicken Man, please don't go to Bien Hoa village. Stay on base where it is safe." I knew that she really liked me, but she did have a boyfriend.

My name had been coming up for sergeant of the guard at night quite a bit lately. It was as if somebody was making sure that I stayed on base at night. As usual, I went from bunker to bunker, checking on the men and what they have seen or heard in front of them. What a mix of guys. Some were all hacked up on caffeine, and some took speed to keep them up. Either way, by the time that I walked into the bunker, they all wanted to talk. At least on quiet nights, it made a twelve-hour shift pass by quickly.

Quiet nights were something we prayed for. Many nights we would get over fifty mortars coming in before they could be stopped. As sergeant of the guard, I had to make serious decisions to protect the men and the berm.

Despite carrying on with everyday life, I was still getting the stomach cramps, so I had been to see the medic again. Once again, I came away with no answer.

However, after a couple of weeks of getting sergeant of the guard every other night, I was told the medics wanted to see me. Standing in line waiting to be seen, I wondered what they could have found wrong with me. Hopefully, they would be able to fix my stomach problem.

The medic informed me that a determination had been made that there was nothing physically wrong with me and that I had mental problems from "too much Vietnam." I was going to be taken to a hospital in Saigon and stay there a few days for evaluation. I did not care, as long as they could do something about my stomach pain. I was given a pill to help me relax and fell asleep in the back of the Jeep ride to Saigon.

Awake in Saigon, I realized I was so sick I could not even stand up. Doctors were fading in and out with color charts wanting to know what I thought the colors represented. When completely awake, I had a hard time talking as I was drooling so much. I don't know what I had been given, but I was really drugged and out of it!

After a couple of days, Bob and a couple of guys from my unit came to see me. They were shocked to see what I looked like. I could hardly talk, was drooling, and could not keep my eyes focused. My lazy eye was completely off. I have always been able to control it, unless I had been drinking, was tired, or on medication.

No wonder they thought that I was crazy. I must have looked crazy with my eyes going in different directions.

After about a week in the hospital in Saigon, I was told by Dr. Jones that if I wanted to, I could go home now on an early out from Vietnam. After all, this was my second tour, and lots of guys got an early out. When I agreed, he said that I would be leaving directly from here and not going back to my unit in Bien Hoa. He insisted again that the pain that I thought I had in my stomach was psychological and to follow the doctor's orders.

I could not believe they would not let me go back to my unit to say goodbye. My personal belongings would be boxed up and shipped home to me. What about Chi? I couldn't even say goodbye to Chi or my men! Was I being punished for something? I was told I would be flown to Fort Ord in California, so from there, I could take a bus home.

I was sedated and soon drifted off to sleep as the medication set in.

I woke up as we landed. I started thinking about how great it would be to go home again, and this time, for good. As I tried to get up, I realized that I could hardly move. Medics were now assisting me in standing, and everything was whirling around. I was almost sick. They walked me off the plane and then into a military ambulance, where I lost consciousness again. When I woke up this time, I was in a hospital bed. I tried to stand but couldn't, so I called for help, and a nurse came and gave me another shot.

Later, when I woke again, I saw guys in all the beds, some moaning, and some looking dead. I asked the guy in the next bed where we were, but he never even responded.

I decided to stand up. As I did, the whole room started to swirl. A nurse came running over and said to lie back down.

Protesting, I demanded to know where I was and when I would be going home.

To my surprise and total shock, I found out that I was in a hospital in Japan, in a psychiatric ward! No wonder the next guy over could not even talk to me. Most guys just sat around or lay staring at the walls. How on earth did I ever wind up here?

A doctor came in every day, telling me to take my medications and giving me more color charts to read. He said I would be here for about a month as they decided where I would go next.

I informed him that Dr. Jones told me that I would be going home on an early out. He said that it did not show on my records and that I had been sent here for thirty days of evaluation. I would be sent back to the world, but where, he did not know yet. I felt like I had become an experimental case. I was given pills constantly, and then they asked me how I was doing on that medication. A particular blue pill made me drool. That was probably the same one that they gave me in Vietnam when I was drooling so bad. One thing about being so heavily drugged is that I had no pain. At least my stomach never hurt.

After a couple of weeks, I realized that I needed to fake taking these pills and spit them out; otherwise, I would be a zombie all day just like everyone else here. I would hold the pills in my mouth, drink the water, and then spit the pills out when the nurse moved on to another patient. In just a couple of days of not taking the pills, I started feeling almost normal. I still faked it in front of the doctors until I figured out what to do next. The doctor said I was doing much better and that I would be sent back to the States in a couple of weeks.

I told Carol, one nurse whom I trusted, about not taking the pills. She said as long as I felt okay, continue. Within a few days, I was informed that I would be leaving in a week for the States. I asked Carol if she would sign me out for a weekend pass so that I could see a little bit of Japan while I was here. She thought that I was doing well enough to let out for a couple of days and agreed. I could only be gone over the weekend, and I must be back before Monday when the doctors come back to work. Carol said I must be careful in Japan, as I would not have any papers authorizing this as I was sneaking out.

I converted some money at the hospital to Japanese yen. Good thing I still had my wallet. The train station was just a short walk, so I boarded a train to Tokyo. I was excited about the weekend with my newfound freedom. I did not want to think about why I was here or what I had been through. I just wanted to enjoy Japan.

Arriving in Tokyo, I realized that I could take a train to Osaka to the World's Fair. The trains were really fast in Japan. I could not find anyone who spoke English but boarded a train to take me to Osaka. After a couple of hours on the train, I finally did find a girl who spoke English, and I found out that I was going the wrong way. I had to catch the next train back to Tokyo.

The two-hour ride back to Tokyo was not as much fun in the dark with nobody to talk to. I paid a cab to take me to the nearest hotel where GIs stay. It was a lively place, as I had expected, with music and girls. Sadly, I was so exhausted from the train trip that after checking in, I had a rice bowl for dinner and went back to my room. Unfortunately, the walls were paper-thin, and people were yelling and dancing all night, so I didn't get much sleep.

The following morning was a little calmer. I took a walk and found the streets were almost empty. It started to rain, so I decided to kick back at the hotel for the day. The bar was full of GIs, so it did not take long to get into a conversation.

Jimmy, a GI from Florida, was on his R&R. We started talking, and he was telling me how much fun it is to take a cab around Tokyo at night. I thought it sounded great but would not want to do it alone. I had already been warned about the older Japanese guys they call "cowboys." These guys are old WWII vets and liked to go out at night and beat up American GIs.

We decided to go together, even though it was still raining. Tokyo at night was amazing. We went to several different bars, ate seafood, and drank sake. So much fun!

The next day was not quite as much fun, since I had to go back and sneak myself back into the hospital. Upon my return, I was informed my orders had been cut for me to prepare to leave for the States. Where, I did not know yet, but I would go anywhere at this point.

CHAPTER 36

MY ORDERS WERE for Fort Ord in California. I was going home. I was so excited I could not believe it was happening to me. California, at last!

I thanked Carol for all she had done for me in Japan. The doctor came in with my instructions and insisted that I take the medications now. I thought, so what? At least I could sleep on the plane. I took the drugs and listened to my medical instructions.

The next thing I remember was waking up in a hospital. As I tried to sit up, I felt as if I were floating in the air. A nurse walking by told me the doctor would be in soon.

"Where am I?"

"Fort Ord, California," she responded.

I made it. I was back in the world.

I could see the doctor through a window looking over my record. He then came in and started showing me color charts right away.

Not again, I thought. This just made me so angry!

"What are you doing? I'm supposed to be getting out on an early out," I started yelling at him. He responded by stomping out of the room. A nurse came in right away and gave me another shot. Once again, the room started swirling, and soon, I was out.

After a long sleep, I awoke to the doctor, shaking me. He said that he had orders for me to report to Fort Lewis, Washington. What the hell? They decided that what I need was an NCO training school?

An NCO school (non-commissioned officer) was a special school for sergeants who the military felt needed more training.

What? Were they truly serious? *More* training? I was already a two-tour Vietnam veteran, Sergeant E5, and I was supposed to be getting an early out.

The following morning after a good night's rest with no shots, I received my orders. They let me get my own transportation, informing me that I was to report immediately to Fort Lewis, Washington.

I was only about a four-hour bus ride to home, where I could pick up my car, so after receiving my orders and having clothes issued, I was on my way to the bus station. Wow, what a great feeling to be free again.

I found out that Mom & Dad were in Montana and would not be home for a couple of weeks. I called Richard to see if he could pick me up from the bus station, and his sister, Gloria, answered the phone. Richard was not in, but she would make sure someone was there to pick me up and take me home. Gloria had really grown up! She was four years younger than I was, making her about fifteen years old. I explained to her that I would not be able to stay long as I needed to report to Fort Lewis, and it would take me a couple of days to get there.

Home, at last! How great to be here. Gloria and her friend, who was driving, drove into my driveway. I immediately saw all of the dogs waiting to greet me. She left me and went to find Richard before I left. I did go to Grandma Emily's trailer and had a beer with her and Aunt Lorean. They were both so excited to see me.

It was so good to be home that I decided to spend the night and leave first thing in the morning, meaning I'd have to drive all the way at once. It would be about fifteen to twenty hours of driving.

Now that I was not taking any medication, I began getting sharp stomach pains again. Oh well, I guess it was just something I was going to need to live with.

My car would not start. It had been parked too long. Luckily, Richard finally came over and then went back to his house and brought back the tractor. He pulled my car down the road with the tractor, and after a couple of minutes, it started running. Black smoke billowed out the back, and it backfired a few times, and then started running a little. I followed Richard over to his house, where we pulled and cleaned the spark plugs. Next, an oil change, and then it was ready to go.

That evening was spent with Richard and Gloria talking about old times and new times. Richard was becoming quite the farmer. Gloria made dinner at their house, and then I went home for a good night's sleep in my own bed. What a treat. Nobody at home, so it made for a nice, quiet night to catch up on my rest.

In the morning, I hit the road, gassed up in Live Oak, and started out for Washington. Once I got to Interstate 5, it was pretty fast moving. I had never been on this new freeway, so it was a bit of an adventure.

I decided to stop for lunch at a truck stop by the Oregon border. As I walked up to the building, a man asked me if I was heading north.

"Actually, I am."

"Could I get a lift to Portland?"

"Okay." I thought at least it would give me somebody to talk with.

After being seated for lunch, he asked me if I could butter? I did not know the term "butter," but I caught it that he was broke. I did not have any extra money but felt obligated, as we had already ordered. After paying the bill, I had about enough money to gas up one more time, so I was not sure if I could make it all of the way to Fort Lewis.

We were only on the road for about an hour when he started acting very weird. He started talking about riots over Vietnam and killing people with his bare hands. It was then that I realized that I might be in trouble. He must be six foot four and at least 280 pounds, early thirties, and very fit. He towered over me!

He started to become very agitated. He was cussing at politicians, police, the military, and just rambling on.

Then he went very quiet for a few moments, and after a pause, said that he had just "killed a guy in Nevada." I wondered if it was the last guy that gave him a ride. He looked over at me with hatred in his eyes. Then, he mentioned that he was just coming on to a "mushroom" that he ate about an hour ago.

Oh no! This guy was out of it on drugs. I realized that I needed a plan, or this could get ugly. If this guy was not lying, he was really a badass, and I made a big mistake by giving him a ride.

I looked in the rearview mirror for any kind of a weapon in my backseat. Nothing but clothes with my army uniform on top. He claimed that he was on his way to Portland, Oregon, to speak at a rally against the war in Vietnam. He said it might get messy there as the Feds and other groups were trying to get him. His anger was rising as he ranted, and his hatred was spilling out.

All of a sudden, he said, "Take the next exit into those trees. I need to take a leak."

I knew then I had to do something. I felt that he was going to attack me and maybe kill me after we stopped. He was talking crazy and rambling on.

So, very calmly, I said, "Jerry, I want to work for you."

"What?"

"I haven't told you about myself. Look at my uniform in the backseat. My voice became stronger. Do you see what's on the arm?"

"Yes, it's the 101st Airborne. So what?"

"In Vietnam, I did search-and-destroy missions, fast hand-to-hand combat. I can kill a man in 4.2 seconds by ripping out his larynx. Jerry, you need me! You already said you wished there was someone else like you. I will be out of the army in two weeks, and I can come work with you. Jerry, nobody can stop us if we work together."

I pulled over, and he was quiet, contemplating my story. I quickly scanned around in the front of the car for anything that I could use as a weapon. Nothing. My heart was racing so fast, I thought it was going to leave me. Without saying a word, he got out of the car to relieve himself. I needed to go as well, but I was not going to take the risk of getting out of the vehicle. He was so big! Me, I am now 5'11" and weigh 140lbs. I would have driven off if he wasn't standing so close to the car.

I was praying that he fell for my story as it was completely made up.

"Let's do it," he agreed.

Back in the car, he started rambling on about some guys in Portland that he would like to take out while he was in town. I could tell his head was now spinning with drugs. On the ride north, I made up stories of killing people in Vietnam and how easy it was.

Now he tells me he is also a Draft Dodger. This guy has no idea how bad I hate a Draft Dodger! A draft dodger is one who has been asked to serve, but does not have the guts to go. Usually, these people will have fake medical problems if they have money or run off to Canada if they are broke.

Finally, a gas station came into sight. A great stop, as I needed a break to think about what to do next. After getting gas and paying for hamburgers for both of us, I was now broke and not sure if I had enough gas to reach Fort Lewis, Washington. I did tell him that I was now broke and needed money for gas, so I was willing to do anything to make some money if he had any ideas. He said he would think about it.

I decided to go on and play the game. I thought he believed me. The rest of the ride was about the same . . . Jerry constantly rambled on about the government or how he wanted to take someone out.

Now I have made a plan if he makes me stop the car one more time. If I must fight him, I really only know one "death blow" that I practiced a lot at Camp Crockett. If he attacks me in the car I will be defenceless. But, if I could get first kick between his legs to weaken him I could go with a straight punch left hand to the nose, right punch downward on the upper part of the nose to break it, and then upper cuts with both fists to the nose to drive it up to his brain! This always worked in training on a dummy, but he is so big!

After what seemed an eternity, we reached Portland city limits. What a welcome sight. It was not far off the freeway when Jerry said, "Stop here."

As I pulled over, he exclaimed, "This is it." Jumping out of the car, he yelled, "Wait here just a minute."

He disappeared into a house, came running back out a few moments later, and got back in the car. I was *really* scared now. I made it through two tours of Vietnam, and now, some nut might kill me. Wow, he handed me his phone number and a twenty-dollar bill.

"Here, this is all the money that I have right now, but I know you need it for gas."

He then got out of the car, this time with his backpack, and simply walked away.

I yelled out, "Thanks for the twenty dollars, Jerry. I'll see you in two weeks."

"Good, let's do it," he yelled back.

I drove off as fast as I could. This nut actually believed me. I was just so relieved that I didn't really have to fight this monster!

What a weirdo. I will never let anybody in my car again!

I was still shaking so bad that I had to stop at the next rest stop and relax for a while. After a short nap in the car, I was back on the road to Fort Lewis. Now, I had enough gas, but I had run out of time, as I was about six hours late for reporting.

As I approached the gate at Fort Lewis, I told the guard that I was late for reporting in and needed to go directly to my assigned unit. He pointed the way and said good luck in an odd way.

I quickly drove over to the barracks as instructed, parked my car, and ran up the stairs. Wow, to my surprise, this looked like basic training. Men were standing by their bunks in their underwear, and this drill instructor was yelling at them like they were all new recruits. He was pulling at their T-shirts, yelling, and pushing. I thought to myself, *He better not touch me when he works his way to me.* Both he and the goon behind him were frowning at me oddly. He was yelling at the top of his voice that we were all here for eight weeks, we were all losers, and it was his job to bring us back to being soldiers—or break us in the process.

He approached me with this look of death, reached out, and grabbed my arm. I knew a blow was following, so I dropped to the floor, pulling his arm with me. He swung, I flipped him and kicked him and his body tumbled backwards down the stairs. We were all stunned and frozen! While I was shocked, my instinct was to run. I leaped over him and landed at the bottom of the stairs. It was like I was flying, as I must have gone twenty feet in the air. All of the men behind me stopped to help the DI, and nobody followed me. I fled, found my car, and quickly drove off the base. As I passed the guard, I waved to him, and when he waved back, I knew that he had not yet received any calls to intercept me.

Now, what to do? I was in Tacoma, Washington. The military police were bound to be looking for me. The DI who went down the stairs may be badly hurt, I didn't know, but I did know that I was in big trouble. I decided I really had no choice but to go back, but I wasn't going to go back to his training!

Okay, if they think I was nuts, I would give them nuts. I was aware that when the doctors gave me drugs, my lazy eye went off, which made me look unquestionably crazy. I could control the eye as long as I was not on alcohol or medication, and I would do just that.

As I approached the gates of Fort Lewis, a guard stepped out.

"I need to report to my unit as they desperately need me right now. My unit is the first of the 327th 101st Airborne Division, working out of Camp Eagle." I looked the guard right in the face with my eyes spread apart!

"What's your name?"

As soon as I told him, Sergeant Travis, he screamed, "Get out of the car!"

As I got out, I told him again desperately, "My unit needs me now."

He demanded, "Where do you think you are?"

"Tan Son Nhut Air Base, Saigon."

"Put your hands in the air and turn around."

He cuffed me, and I stood there as he called someone on his radio. Soon, a military ambulance pulled up, and security guards strapped me inside the ambulance, where a nurse proceeded to give me a shot.

I awoke in the psychiatric ward. It was morning, and the doctor was trying to talk to me. He had been studying my charts and did not understand why I was ever sent to Fort Lewis. He also informed me the officer I knocked down the stairs was really hurting but would be okay and was demanding my return as soon as possible. He will be wearing a neck brace for a while but he will live, it could have been worse!

"You know that you can't go back into his unit?"

I replied, "I know. The drill instructor will probably kill me."

"Yes, he will," the doctor agreed. He also said that I should leave this base as soon as possible! He claimed the DI was known to be a real badass and he will get even!

"I'm going to have orders cut right away for you to report to the hospital in Fort Ord, California. You should leave within the hour if you know what's good for you."

"Oh, I understand, and I thank you. But what about my car?"

He said it would be waiting for me in front of the hospital.

Before leaving the base, I had to go to finance and get gas money to make it back to Fort Ord. I was so worried that the DI would catch up to me with some of his goons, but he did not. He must have still been in a Hospital bed?

As I drove off the base this time, it felt like such a relief, even though I did not know what was in front of me except a long drive back to Fort Ord, California. Of course, this time, I would not be picking up any hitchhikers.

I drove straight home, where I had decided to overnight, only stopping for gas. It was twelve hours of driving. I was so exhausted that I didn't let anyone know that I was home. I did go over to Grandma Emily's trailer for a quick beer. Mom & Dad were still in Montana but due back any day. The following morning, I was up early and on the road to Fort Ord.

CHAPTER 37

As I DROVE the next four hours, I started thinking about my life. What was happening, and where I was going? I still did not know how I ever ended up in Japan. Who would have ever sent me to a psycho ward? The pain in my stomach was real—at least to me. It did hurt!

I wondered about Kenny over in Vietnam, if he was still alive?

Arriving at the gates of Fort Ord, I tried to decide what to do. I was furious by now at my situation. I was a Sergeant E5, I had served two tours in Vietnam, and I was being treated like a new recruit or psycho. I didn't even know what to think of myself anymore?

As I handed the guard my orders, he gave me a strange look and pointed me toward the hospital. I found a parking spot a few blocks away and hoped the car didn't get towed if I was here for a while.

When I handed the hospital my orders, I was sent straight to the psychiatric ward. A nurse took my vital signs and handed me two pills to relax me. I took the pills, wondering why I needed to be relaxed.

I woke up in a hospital bed, once again feeling dizzy and disorientated. A nurse instructed me to take more pills and said that I would be seeing a doctor later. Here we go again . . . I took the pills and fell back asleep.

The doctor was shaking me, trying to wake me. He walked away, telling the nurse to let him know as soon as I was alert. I sat up, and the nurse served me a cup of coffee. Wow, this was the first time that I had ever been served coffee like this in a hospital. She quickly went after the doctor.

When the doctor returned, he asked me, "Do I look familiar?"

I said, "Yes, you do." I did recognize him but wasn't sure from where.

"I gave orders to release you months ago in Vietnam."

He was my doctor in Vietnam, Dr. Jones. He was the doctor who said I would be going home on an early out.

"What are you still doing in the army?"

I told him about waking up in Japan, spending a month there. I felt like I was a test monkey for new drugs. Then I told him about Fort Lewis, Washington, and what happened there. He was not happy to hear what happened to me and said that he wanted a couple of hours to look into this. I walked over to the cafeteria and read a local newspaper, catching up on the world.

When I returned, he apologized for what had happened to me. He was so sorry. He claimed that he did cut orders for me to get an early out and did not know what happened. He said that only a General could override his orders and asked me if any General was out to get me for anything? He said the file had been closed so he could not get any information about who had countermanded his orders. I didn't know what to say; so I said nothing, Wow, could General Abrams do this to get even with me for when I brought Kenny out of the field? I don't want to believe that.

Putting passed events aside, he said, "I have the authority to re-lease you right away. An early out, just like I told you in Vietnam. You qualify, and I can send you home tomorrow."

I was in shock! It was finally over. I would be going home on February 23, 1971.

The next morning, I received my orders of discharge, travel pay, and my final paycheck. Dr Jones also authorized an additional $1,500 to me for severance pay, which equalled ten years' worth of disability of 10 percent, as he put on my DD 214. He said I deserved this disability for what happened to me in Japan. He apologized again for what had happened to me since leaving Vietnam. I believed that he really felt sorry for what had happened . . . or maybe he knew more than he was telling me?

I was glad to see that my car was still there waiting for me. The four-hour drive home was so much fun, knowing that I was now free—what a feeling. I thought back on what might have happened to me leaving Vietnam, and the only person who might have contacted General Abrams would have been that warrant officer who I gave the top-secret blank envelope to, as he knew something was not right. Even if General Abrams found out, I found it hard to believe that he would send me to Japan as a test monkey for new drugs. That was inhumane, and I didn't want to believe it, so I didn't.

Chapter 38

IT WAS MUCH different coming home than I expected. Mom & Dad were happy that I was back, but I could feel that things were not the same. The pain in my stomach was still there, almost daily, so Mom called Dr. Bartchi, who had been our family doctor for many years.

After my visit to his office, I found out that he had told my mother in confidence that he felt that I had spent too much time in Vietnam and had been affected by it. I was not pleased to hear that another doctor "thinks I'm a lunatic."

Nevertheless, I was not going to let this bother me, so I tried calling Joy, who I used to date in high school, thinking we could catch up. I spoke with her sister, who informed me that Joy was married. Joy was gone! What other girls could still be here that I know? I called Sharon from Live Oak, only to find that she had moved away! I think she got married? I had no other girls to call so I called Richard and spent the evening with him. We drove around his latest orchards that he acquired and had big laughs as we talked about past times. He claimed he laughs every time he thinks about us going to Reno with him dressed up in that military uniform. We had some of the best times growing up together!

The next day, I found out from Mom that a letter had been sent from the US Army saying that when I was released from the military, I would never be the same. I would be coming home with "mental problems" from Vietnam. She could not find the letter, so I didn't know who wrote it, but they were definitely out to destroy me!

Of course, my mom could not hold a secret, so all of the family had read the letter, but nobody knew where it was. My family now thought that I was nuts! How embarrassing! I could tell by the looks and comments that even my sisters thought I was a "deranged Vietnam veteran."

One of my nieces told me what the family was saying behind my back. I felt devastated . . . The kids (my nieces and nephews) have been told never to be alone with Ike! What? The feeling of being removed from the family where I had been so loved and wanted as a boy . . . I realized right away that I couldn't stay home any longer. I wanted to run. I had to escape somewhere, but I just didn't know where. To have family members look at me and think I was nuts was too much to bear. Mom & Dad wanted me to live at home and go to college, but I knew I had to go. No one else would tell me the truth except my one niece!

I called Bob, my friend from Vietnam, whom I travelled to Hong Kong with. He had just returned from Vietnam, and he also was now out of the military. He was staying with his parents in an old hotel they had purchased in Bend, Oregon. He did not know anyone in Bend except his parents, so he had no ties to the area.

He came up with a suggestion. "Why don't you drive up here, spend a few days with me, and we'll decide where to go next? Maybe Hawaii?"

We could draw unemployment and get our checks sent to us in any state, including Hawaii. I had the money to do this as I had almost $5,000 total.

That sounded great to me, as I was ready to go anywhere.

My parents were not happy that I was leaving again so soon. I didn't think they would ever understand my situation and how hard it was for me. Dad would have been much happier if I would live with them and go hunting and fishing like we used to.

I was only home for five days before I left. The drive to Bend, Oregon, was about ten hours, but I never got tired as I had so much going through my head.

Bob was very pleased to see me, and I could tell that his parents were hoping that we would go somewhere together. His parents were not nearly as loving as mine, and they did not even want Bob to live with them. They were people of money and liked to do their own thing without their adult children. They did have one good story that I liked. It was about how they met. Bob's mother was the "maid" to the father and his first wife before she died.

After a couple of days in Bend, driving around and reminiscing about Vietnam, we decided we were ready to go to Hawaii.

We booked our flight and prepared to leave within a couple of days. On the plane, we were so excited that neither one of us could stop talking. The people around us on the plane were all tourists going to Hawaii for the week, but we were going for an indefinite time. At the airport, we looked through the local newspaper and chose an apartment right across from Waikiki Beach.

Living in Hawaii, and especially Waikiki, was tons of fun. We would meet new people almost every day. Most people we met were tourists and were there only for a few days. The bus system was the best. For only fifty cents, you could ride all over the island. That made it so easy to get around that we would only rent a car about once a week.

During my first week in Waikiki, I was walking down Kalakaua Avenue when I recognized my childhood neighbor, Marsha, Richard's older sister. We were very shocked to see each other. She was in Hawaii on vacation. What a small world!

As the days went on, my pain became worse, and I just didn't feel right. Finally, after about 10 months in Hawaii, I told Bob that

I wanted to go home, or at least back to the mainland. I didn't see a doctor in Hawaii as I feared they would only tell me that I was nuts.

It took us a couple of weeks to get our air tickets and pack up. We had made several friends in Hawaii who wanted us to stay, and we would have, if I wasn't so sick. I am now throwing up daily!

Once back on the mainland, Bob and I rented an apartment in Salem, Oregon. I still refused to see another doctor. We met several girls right away from eating at different restaurants. I was dating Merry for about a month, a girl I met through one of our friends at a restaurant, when she told me she was pregnant. She has just missed her period. The next day, she claimed to have gone to the doctor and found that she was pregnant. I felt it was my duty to marry her, as the child was mine, so surely, it was meant to be!

Merry was initially from Lincoln City, Oregon, and her family's house was right on the beach. We planned our wedding and married in Lincoln City about a month later.

Merry and I moved to Portland, Oregon, and I got a job as assistant manager of a finance company. I really enjoyed living in Portland, but the pain in my stomach was getting worse by the day. Merry also had a hard time, as she bled every day. She said the doctor told her that was normal, but at times blood would be running down her leg.

Finally, about six months later, I had no choice. I was in so much pain that I could not take it any longer. I went to the VA Hospital in Portland, Oregon. The VA looked at my records and informed me that the only way they would admit me was in the psychiatric ward. I agreed, as long as they would stop the pain.

The patients in the psychiatric ward always looked the same. There was no conversation. Nobody spoke. They just lay in bed with blank faces.

Once again (this was too familiar), I was given a handful of pills, and off to sleep I went. This hospital was different, however, because every day, a new intern would come into my room and run tests on me for whatever they were studying to become. After about a week, a man named Dr. Potter came in. He was studying to be a kidney specialist. He asked me when the last time was that I had my kidneys checked. I didn't know if anyone had ever checked them as the pain was in my front, not my back.

He took me into x-ray and said that I would be on the table for about twenty minutes. After about an hour, I asked the attendant what was wrong. He said he only takes the x-rays; he didn't read them. A little later, Dr. Potter came back.

He took me into another room where an entire wall was full of my x-rays. They showed one functional kidney and one "dead" one. He explained that I needed to have the dead kidney removed immediately.

Dr. Potter had me call my parents, who were in Montana on a deer hunting trip. Mom flew out to Portland that night. The operation was scheduled for the next day.

As I was being prepped for surgery that morning, they noticed that my blood pressure was over 300. The surgeon stopped the operation and gave me blood pressure medication. It did not work. The surgeon then refused to operate; as he was worried I would have a stroke or might not know my own name, if I even lived through it. They had me on a bed in intensive care, waiting to find a surgeon who would perform the operation.

The next day, by chance, a surgeon from Lettermen Hospital, San Francisco, flew up for a brain surgery. My mom sat with the guy's wife during the four-hour operation. This surgeon agreed to do my operation the same day, no matter what the blood pressure count read.

I was prepped and ready. As soon as the surgeon walked in, he started shouting orders. Nurses were moving quickly. The last thing I remember was a nurse telling him that my blood pressure was still over 200. I heard the doctor say, "Put him under now."

I woke up about six hours later with the surgeon asking me my name. As soon as I told him, he walked out. I later found out that when I said my name, he knew I had come through okay. He was needed right away in San Francisco for another surgery. I never did see him again.

THE OTHER SIDE OF NAM

During this time, Merry lost the baby as she had a twisted uterus. Then she admitted the baby was not mine! We had a marriage annulment a few months later.

Eighteen months after being discharged from the army, I had a kidney removed at Portland VA hospital and was told the kidney had been "dead for at least two years," putting me in Vietnam with the 101st Airborne. I didn't know what happened to me in Vietnam, but one thing I did know . . . *I was not crazy!*

I really was in pain for two years with a dead kidney inside of me—and nobody believed me!

How lucky I was and thankful to be alive!

Epilogue

It had been thirty years since I've been to Vietnam—thirty years and one month—and now I could see the coastline in the distance, as we got closer. I was coming back for the first time on a cruise ship into Hạ Long Bay, North Vietnam. The only way that I thought that I would ever see North Vietnam was as a prisoner of war, and, now, here it was. I was entering North Vietnam!

Kenny had called me a couple of weeks earlier and told me that I should cancel my trip. He claimed that if the NVA (North Vietnamese Army) found out that I was a Vietnam veteran, they would kill me. I told him no way was that happening. The times and the people had changed, and tours were now developing all over Vietnam. They wanted us back, and of course, they wanted American money.

The ship had mostly Chinese tourists and our group of about eighty Americans. My cabinmate was Jay from Sacramento, and he and I already had a "wild night" in Hong Kong. I forgot to tell Jay about the Tea Girls, and after a couple of beers, he found out his tab was over $200. Every girl that walked by him said, "Will you buy me a tea"? He learned quickly—but not quick enough. Wow, how the price of tea had changed!

The large cruise ship, *Star Cruises*, could not dock in Hạ Long Bay, so we had to tender in. As our tender pulled up to the dock, I could see about 100 Vietnamese standing there to greet us. As the passengers started to disembark, I could hear the Vietnamese counting, "*Mot, Hai, Ba, Bon*," and I started counting with them. I was so excited! Then I realized that all eyes were on me counting in their language. I realized that I might have made a big mistake.

As I stepped off the tender, a man stepped in front of me and said, "I am an NVA." My heart dropped to my waistline for a moment, and then he said, with his hand extended, "I am your tour guide, and my name is Cuong."

I was shocked *and* excited. He asked me what unit I was with in Vietnam.

I said, "In the field, the 101st Airborne."

He smiled and said, "Good, we will talk later."

About sixty passengers and I were on a tour of the many islands, about 3,000, off the coast of Hạ Long Bay. During the afternoon, Cuong and I became friends. We shared stories, laughter, and tears. Many of the passengers took pictures of Cuong and I standing together.

His stories were shocking, with the way that they lived and died fighting for their country. The Vietnam War was known to the Vietnamese, and still is, as "The American War."

Cuong was only fifteen years old when he became an NVA. He was picked up walking a street in Hanoi. His unit of twenty-five men crossed into South Vietnam to fight the Americans. They crossed over from North Vietnam with no identification on them. They were provided with no supplies of food and were forced to live off the land.

Cuong was there during the end of the war. Out of twenty-five men in the beginning, they were down to seventeen. Most had died from fighting the Americans, but a couple had died of illness and starvation. They were having trouble finding anything to eat and getting too weak to travel. They were on the coastline and could see the fishing boats with their nets out but could also see the US patrol boats guarding them. Cuong told the men that being the youngest of them, he could swim out to the boats and try to cut into the nets and grab a couple of large fish.

It was very dark when Cuong entered the water. He swam out to the boats and quickly cut into the nets. Yes, they were full of fish. As he grabbed a couple of fish, he realized that bullets were zinging through the water, meaning the patrol boats were on to him. He went deep into the water and was hoping that he was heading toward the shore. He finally had to come up for air and found that he was, indeed, going in the right direction. The boat crew thought he was still by the nets, so they fired more rounds into the water. They did not know he was already heading to shore. He dove back deep into the water, and then a bullet struck him. As his head came out of the water, he realized that bullets did not hit him, but he was being gouged by bamboo!

He saw that his comrades were linking together to try to reach him, but he must somehow get over the bamboo first. He found a broken one for his foot to stand on and plunged toward his comrades onshore. Cuong missed by about two feet and landed on the bamboo. His comrades pulled him in. He was bleeding from all of the bamboo punctures. Cuong raised his two hands. He still had two large fish! The men quickly pulled him over the hilltop so that they would not be spotted. They had no time to rest, as the patrol boats would have already alerted troops on land to be looking for them. They ate the fish raw and then ran into the mountains where they knew they could hide and rest.

Soon after that, word spread quickly that the US had pulled out of Vietnam. The Vietnam War was over April 30, 1975.

I applied three times in thirty-two years for veterans' benefits and was always told that my records were "missing." Finally, thirty-two years later, I was granted a board meeting in San Francisco. At that meeting, I was informed that my records were *not* missing; only misplaced. They had studied my dead kidney when it was removed and concluded that the kidney died from "blunt force trauma," and I should have died instantly! Later, I met with a Chief of Staff who informed me that I do have PTSD for many reasons including: I have no memory of the incident that destroyed my kidney. He also said that was probably for the best and to let it go. He did say that something happened in Saigon at the hospital as I was given a "very bad diagnosis," but no other information was available. I will never know the truth.

I will always wonder who sent me to a "psycho ward" in Japan and who sent that horrible letter to my family?

Kenny dies of Agent Orange-related cancer.
Kenneth Lloyd Denney
1949–2015

Kenneth Lloyd Denney was born in Marysville, California, on December 12, 1949, to Lloyd George Denney and Nora Bell Hartman. Kenneth loved camping, gold panning, cross-country skiing, and photography. He grew up in Marysville, where he attended Marysville High School and later lived as a Yuba County resident for over fifty years. Prior to entering the U.S. Army for his first tour in Vietnam, he achieved his GED. Kenneth served two tours in Vietnam as an infantryman in the U.S. Army and later as a door gunner on a helicopter. Kenneth received several accommodations, including the U.S. Air Medal for completing over twenty-five missions in four months as a door gunner. After serving in the army, Kenneth enlisted and served in the U.S. Navy on the USS *Enterprise* for an additional four years as a radio operator. Kenny told me that he had told our story of him with "Top-Secret Orders in Vietnam" all over the world, and even though most people thought it to be an amazing story, not one person ever believed it! He continued his service after the military by first working as a fire spotter for the U.S. Forest Service and later retiring from the U.S. Postal Service after twenty years of service.

Richard dies of a heart attack
Richard Rolufs Wilson
1951–2016

Richard was born on April 25, 1951. His parents, Jack and Rosemary (Mayfield) Wilson, lived and raised him and his sisters, Marsha and Gloria, on their farm in Live Oak. His boyhood was spent working on the farm. He graduated from Live Oak High in 1969. Richard loved camping, hunting, farming, and fast cars! His dream was to be a farmer all of his life. As an adult, Richard became a very successful farmer of prunes, almonds, and rice. Richard and his wife Jeannie lived on his grandfather's ranch. Also living on the ranch was Jacque, Richard's second wife who worked the orchards during harvest and became part of the family. Richard was very well known in the farming community and made a mark in farming that will be remembered for many years to come! Richard and Jeannie never had children, but Richard did have a daughter with a longtime girlfriend, Debbie, and a son with his first wife, Sheila. His daughter, Jennifer, will continue his farming legacy!

About the Author

Ike Travis is a retired sales executive from the hospitality industry. In his younger years after Vietnam, Ike worked in the casino business, and in just a few years, became a casino manager. He was the casino manager for Costa Cruises on cruise ships in the Caribbean. Ike was also the casino manager of the Cal Neva Lodge at Lake Tahoe, the same resort hotel that Frank Sinatra once owned. It was there that he met his future wife, Manette Belliveau. Manette and Ike were together for thirty years before she passed away in 2012 from breast cancer. Manette became the founding President/CEO of Visit Oakland! It was her wish for Ike to complete this book. They had no children due to Manette fighting breast cancer for twenty-one years. At sixty-one years old, Ike retired and now resides in Brookings, Oregon.

CPSIA information can be obtained
at www.ICGtesting.com
Printed in the USA
LVHW090405281021
701751LV00001B/50